It'll be okay

ACCEPTANCE, CHOICES, DELIVERANCE

EMMA

P POWERFUL
BOOKS

Contents

My Letter

*D*ear Mini Me,

    This book, these words are for you. This is our story. Our life. It's going to be a hard read for you, I think. But persevere. I promise it'll be worth it. I know you're feeling pain right now, and I know you'll feel more pain than you thought possible while going on this journey, but trust me when I tell you, amongst all the hard, the heartbreak and the soul shattering moments, there will also be moments, periods of time, when you laugh. When you realise the hard stuff is far outweighed by the good. We live for the good stuff. We are a good person. We thrive on making people smile, making them happy. Not for any other reason than because it makes us happy. We know right from wrong, and we strive to always do the right thing. Now. It hasn't always been that way. But now, it absolutely is that way.

    It's important you know, you can't have a rainbow without a little rain, and we have the brightest, shiniest rainbow I have ever seen.

    So, grab yourself a milkshake, and settle down. This may be hard but like I said, it'll be worth it.

    You are amazing. And you are so very loved. As you read these words, understand that. You. Are. Loved.

    Love always, the older, slightly, more wrinkled version of you!

Message from Emma

The following words are my story. It's my life up until this point. It's been hard to write and even harder to read back through. But I felt it was time and if I can help just one person to realise they are deserving of happiness, love, and friendship, then me purging all of this, is worth it for me. I'm not an author by any stretch of the imagination, but what I am, is a person who has been through varying different degrees of trauma and come through it the other side a pretty decent person. You can go through shit, and work out it wasn't your fault, it wasn't because of anything you did or didn't do, not because of something you did or didn't say. You are a good person. You have found or come across my book for a reason. As contrite as it sounds, I came into your life for a reason. Read my words, hear my story, take from it what you will. But please know, you can, and you will get through this.

It's important for me that as a reader, you remember that I'm not an author. I'm a person who has a story to tell. I have been through various different situations, and I've come through the other side of them all. I still struggle daily, but I choose my path. You can too. By choosing your path, you choose which way you want to live your life. My chapters are a little wonky, some are long, some are short. But every single one of them is a part of me.

CHAPTER ONE

"GOD, GRANT ME THE SERENITY TO ACCEPT THE THINGS I CANNOT CHANGE, THE COURAGE TO CHANGE THE THINGS I CAN, AND THE WISDOM TO KNOW THE DIFFERENCE."

God gives his hardest battles to his strongest warriors. That's how the saying goes, or something like that anyway. But I don't want to be a warrior anymore. I want to hand back my shield and sword, my armour, and get a refund. But here's the funny thing, I don't have a choice. I have to find the strength from somewhere. I have a husband now. Two beautiful children who are my world.

I honestly didn't think I'd ever get to this point. The point where I have two little humans dependant on me. Life has a funny way of giving you things that will have a hugely positive impact on your life just when you think everything is going to shit. This book is going to be full of pain, sadness, hurt, and honesty. It may hurt some people who know me, should they read it. That is not, nor has it ever been my intention.

This book is going to show you, how you too, can be the very strongest, most resilient version of yourself regardless of what you've had thrown at you. I want to tell you how I kicked all the bad in the balls, brushed off my crown, and became strong. And happy. Don't get me wrong, I still have days when shit is just... hard. Cripplingly hard. I allow myself to feel it, then I put it back in its box, and take one more step forward. Read my story, take from it what you will, but read it all. You can't have a rainbow without a little rain. I need you to come through my rainstorm with me, so we can dance in the puddles at the end.

CHAPTER TWO

"LIFE IS NOT A PROBLEM TO BE SOLVED, BUT A REALITY TO BE EXPERIENCED." — SOREN KIERKEGAARD.

U p until I was sixteen, I was one of those kids that ardently believed your virginity was to be kept sacred until your wedding night. Simple. I also believed, probably more strongly, we were all sent to this place called Earth, to serve a purpose. Whatever that was, however that looked, we served our purpose and then we died and went home. A simple mindset, but in the eyes of my blissfully naïve self, it worked, and it was something I lived by. An ethos I was hugely private about and incredibly proud of.

I went to an all-girl private boarding school. I'd hated it with a passion. I was the fat kid with glasses and a bad haircut, it was a longer version of the bowl cut, but with uncontrolled curls. Add into all of that, my family home was literally five minutes down the road. The problem with that? I was a full-time boarder. I was a target for all those "pretty rich girls". You know the ones. They have the perfect hair, skinny – or what the fat kid deemed skinny anyway – and they made my life utter misery. I was pushed down the stairs to see if I'd bounce at the bottom, I was poked with sharp objects to see if I'd burst. You get the idea. School for me was quite simply, shit. I hated it and all I wanted was to fit in and have friends. So, I did what any adolescent would do. I tried hard to befriend this particular group, when that ultimately didn't work, I tried making friends with other groups.

There was a particular group who were considered "rebels". This was the group I found myself in. I honestly don't know if they felt sorry for me, or if they liked me, but here I was, finally, with friends.

There was a particular spot in the school grounds we called the "day girls' camp". It was literally a hollowed out Rhododendron bush. The way you went in, was the same way you left. We'd go there in groups and just hang out. The school backed onto a local housing estate, so we frequently had visitors in our little hang out. They were all local boys, and it soon became quite the thing for us to do. And honestly, a lot of fun. We'd meet up during lunch break sometimes, but mostly after school had finished. We'd stay for hours sometimes, and very quickly became good friends with this group of boys. Let's be honest though, when you've been targeted and bullied by your own peers, made to feel like the most revolting thing on the planet, being shown a little attention by some boys, did my confidence the world of good, even if it was only for a little while. In the sanctity of this hollowed out bush, I felt special. Like I belonged.

In 1993, I was sixteen and getting ready to sit my GCSE's. I had decided to study and prove all my teachers wrong. They were all convinced I was going to epically fail everything. I wanted to show them I did have a brain underneath the bad haircut. I hadn't been to meet the boys all term. Dammit, I had a point to prove, and I was going to do it.

On the 14th June 1993, I got word four of the boys were in our little camp and they wanted to see me. I was told they'd missed me and wanted to say hi. I explained I couldn't go down because I was revising, and the girl who'd come up to relay this message to me, was asked to tell them sorry, but no. She was insistent. I think back on it now, how special it made me feel. How wanted. Not in a sexual way, but I finally had friends and they wanted to see me because they'd missed me being around. So, I went down to say hi.

What happened next, changed my life forever.

It was a Monday, about seven thirty in the evening. I had changed out of my school uniform and was wearing black leggings, a white t-shirt, and a blue lumberjack type shirt. I had on cheap knock-off Timberland boots with the laces undone. It wasn't quite dark yet, but it was drizzling. I remember because the wet was refreshing on my face.

When I got down to the camp, I saw the four boys. And that's what they were, boys. They were thirteen and fourteen years old. The older boys we used to hang out with, hadn't come up that night, just the younger ones. There were no other girls there. I didn't think anything of it then. Why would I? They were my friends and they wanted to see me. They wouldn't hurt me.

I went in and saw them standing there. Once I was clear of the entrance/exit, I felt more than saw two of them move to block the exit. So desperate was I to make friends, I quickly shooed away the warning bells. Until I heard one sentence.

"Emma, can we rape you?"

One sentence that completely turned my world on its axis. I had come to know these boys over the last couple of years. I'd trusted them, I'd given them part of my heart. We'd laughed and shared so much together. Friends don't ask their friends to do this. To share something of themselves they hold so dear. This one question completely removed any and all semblance of trust I had. It made me realise people aren't actually your friends.

I remember sitting on the nearest tree trunk, crossing my arms over my chest, and crossing my legs over each other so tightly it hurt. If you don't know something is coming, you aren't afraid, you aren't anxious. But when you know something is about to happen, something so big it's going to completely alter your course, your path in life, you're afraid. You're more frightened than you ever thought possible. Up until then, I didn't know this sort of terror existed.

I remember it all. As if it happened yesterday. The hands, the sneers, the smells, the touches that should have been forbidden, but were, at this moment, fair game. I remember hearing belt buckles and zippers, the sound of my t-shirt and leggings being torn. My underwear shredded as if it were nothing but a scrap of paper. I remember becoming suddenly aware of how green the leaves on the bushes were, there were still flowers attached to the branches in all their beauty. A beautiful pink colour, perfectly formed flowers almost laughing at me. They were untouched, they would remain beautiful, flawless. I had suddenly become broken, soiled.

I couldn't scream, I couldn't cry. I had nothing, no emotion would surface. I said "no" on repeat. I know I said it out loud, it may have been quiet, but they heard me. I knew they'd heard me. I felt them so close to me, it felt like their whole body was entering mine. Two of them had violated me in the worst possible way. Taking my virginity that I held so dear, taking with them all the beliefs I had. That day, on the 14th June 1993, these boys ripped my heart and soul from my body, and I had no idea how to get it back.

Just as the other two boys were getting into position, something in me snapped. I kicked, clawed, and bit my way out of the sacred camp, knowing I would never go back there. It was both sad and joyous. A bittersweet moment. I had escaped from the hell I had just endured, but I also knew I'd never go back to the first place I felt like I'd belonged to.

I ran, to me, I felt if I didn't run, they may try to chase me and finish what they'd started. I ran back up to the school building, shirt hanging off one shoulder, t-shirt torn awkwardly up the middle, and leggings shredded in the crotch area. I was missing a boot, and I still have no idea where it went. Oddly enough, I remember looking down at my feet later on and wondering where and at what point I'd lost it. I remember being really sad about this one missing boot, as they were my favourite pair and damn nearly the only pair of shoes I had at school other than my school shoes. Let's be honest, no one wants to wear a pair of polished school brogues with their normal home clothes.

I don't remember the events that happened next. The memories I do have are not my own. They are memories I've retained from information other people have given me. My dad told me he'd been called up to the school close to midnight. Him and my mum spent time with the headmaster and apparently the headmaster said the word "penis" in excess of twelve times. No one in that meeting ever said the word rape. As far as my parents were aware, I had been sexually assaulted, but even then, that came from me. I have no idea what they had been told, probably that I was a nightmare student and everything that had happened, had ultimately been my fault. I hated that school. With a passion and fierceness I had never felt before. It became a rage that very nearly consumed me.

I was expelled from school because I was raped. The headmaster of the school made several implications the rape was my fault. Because I'd invited the boys up before, this time must have been my doing as well. Doesn't matter I told them my truth, they didn't believe it. I had to sit my exams segregated from everyone else, and I had to be escorted on and off the school grounds each day. I was expelled with such speed I hadn't had a chance to pack any of my stuff up. My clothes, uniform, personal belongings. So, as I waited to be collected after another exam, I decided to take it upon myself to whip up to my old dormitory and pack my own belongings up. Well shit, I don't think I'd ever seen members of staff move as quickly as they did that day. I had an adult – two of the most intimidating teachers in the school – on each arm, and I was physically removed from the building with a warning to not ever come back. I still don't remember what happened to my stuff.

When I said I was segregated from the rest of my peers, that wasn't really correct. I was treated like a leper. Like I had some sort of horrific disease. Almost as if I even so much as looked at anyone, then I would pass on my "dirty" to them.

My parents, as much as I love them, were misled. They weren't told the truth that night. I don't actually know what they were told, I just believe they were under the impression I was sexually assaulted because that had been a choice I'd made. That was hard enough for them to deal with, and I didn't want them to hurt any more than they were already. So, I hid the truth, I silenced my voice and went along for the ride. They simply didn't know how to deal with this new horror in front of them. I tried to make it as easy as I could for them. I was "fine" from then on. It was an easy choice to make. Their happiness was everything for me. Still is. Some would think that may be a misguided or naïve mindset. It's how I was though.

I found out the school did get the police involved, against my wishes. The police never came to speak to me, but the boys had "attempted rape" put on their records. I have no idea how that worked because I never went to court and

I didn't press charges. According to someone I spoke to, I don't remember who, they were too young to have been charged with rape. I never did understand that, but it is etched in my memory.

CHAPTER THREE

"DON'T LET YESTERDAY TAKE UP TOO MUCH OF TODAY." — WILL ROGERS.

I had the whole of the summer holidays to get my shit together before I started sixth form. The whole getting my shit together? It was short lived. As soon as I started sixth form college, I suddenly realised all bets were off. Oh. My. God. Boys, alcohol, weed, no parents and an absolute free for all. Sounds amazing, right? To most people it would have been. But this was the beginning of what turned out to be my very impressive (my parents didn't agree) downfall. A slippery slope I simply had fuck all control over.

My parents did their level best to help, but in their world, helping wasn't talking about it or not asking questions you simply might not want the answers to. That was just the way it was for us. The way that they were raised, and in turn the way I was raised. You just get on with it and deal. Simple. But it wasn't that simple. Not for me. My head bandits had taken root and were growing daily. Getting stronger in silence.

I didn't know how to deal with the mess inside my head, so I started rebelling. Doing things deliberately to get attention. It wasn't that I craved attention, I wanted to "fit in", I wanted to be liked, and honestly at that point, I didn't know how to be someone's friend. I didn't know who I was and what I liked, I found out what other people wanted and liked and manipulated myself to become that. Just so that I could have a friend.

All the time I was trying to manage my own thoughts and fears of failure, I was having the same horrific night terror every single night. The rape all over again. Every detail, every sound, touch, and smell. Relived in the one place I was supposed to feel safe. When I was asleep. Suffice to say, I didn't feel truly at ease even in sleep.

My parents were none the wiser to any of this. My apparent promiscuity, the night terrors, none of it. That's what happens when you have mental health issues, and you go to boarding school. You become secretive, learn to wear a mask, and wear it well. They knew something was up I think, either that or they just thought therapy might be a good idea. It was, however, my choice to hide it from them. I own that choice 100%. I didn't want them to feel any kind of pain or negative feeling around what had happened to me and the choices I made in the years following.

I started seeing a woman in the local town to my school. I had to learn how to open up and be less secretive, how to trust someone. Not an easy thing to do at all. My last session with her was one I remember with some clarity. I had told her that my night terrors had changed slightly. Still the same assault, smells, touches, and sounds, but instead of being able to see faces, people, all of a sudden those faces and bodies were wearing what I call a Grim Reaper cloak. You know, the massive black cloaks with the hood? Those, and all I could see now, were eyes. My delightful therapist told me very casually that the dream had changed because it meant it was going to happen again.

I don't remember an awful lot from that year at sixth form. I'm not sure why, but I believe that one's brain tends to be selective with memories once you've had a trauma. There were a few people who did have an impact on me, I remember them and their names, but they aren't really people that I would want to be in touch with now. I was in a bad place back then, and now I simply choose who gets to be around me.

I was asked to leave that sixth form college. My mum and Dad being told I didn't have the "intellectual capacity" for A levels. Yet another thing to add to the shit list of things I'm apparently crap at. My parents decided to send me to a sixth form college over in Canada as a last ditch attempt to get me some qualifications.

In the UK, turning eighteen is a big deal. It's when you can vote, and more importantly, when you can drink alcohol legally. But I turned eighteen the weekend I arrived at this new school overseas. Most kids would think themselves really lucky and dare I say it, privileged, to go to school in Canada. But I didn't feel like that. I saw myself as a problem that needed to go away. My brother, in my eyes, was the golden child. He was the one that always did everything right. In my head, as twisted as it sounds, my parents didn't love me nearly as much as they loved my brother. So, they shipped me away. Out of sight, out of mind.

I hated this Canadian school. More than hate, this place felt like my own personal living Hell. I met a few people who I thought I liked. I tried desperately to fit in. Again. Be what I thought people wanted me to be. The party animal, the go getter, the shy quieter person, the dare devil. I'd manipulate my own personality to "fit" into whatever situation came up.

It didn't work. So, I decided I was going to do whatever I needed to in order to go home. I missed my parents terribly. I'd never actually been homesick before, so this was a completely new concept for me, and I didn't really know what to do with this new feeling of emptiness. Regardless of how I thought my parents' thought about me, I knew how I felt, and I wanted to go home and be around people and places I knew.

I started going out after "lights out". I'd go into the local town and to the nightclub there. I couldn't tell you anything about it, memories from that time are really patchy, but I knew I became a drug dealer of sorts. A tiny, minuscule, and insignificant person. With no real standing. I don't even think I was ever actually a proper dealer. Just someone who would hand out whatever was needed at the time. I remember stuffing packets in my bra at one point.

Anyway, someone from the school would realise where I was and come and get me, it was a free taxi ride back to the dormitory, I wasn't going to argue.

One morning, I got called out of lessons and taken to the principal's office. She sat me down and told me I'd got what I'd wanted and I was being expelled and sent home. I was equal parts elated and terrified. I now had to call my mum and tell her I was being put on a plane home.

I don't remember packing up my stuff, getting to the airport or boarding the plane. I do remember seeing my mum in London on the other side of security. The hug and then the silent drive home. When we got home, my mum told me, "Your father is waiting for you in the study."

I damn nearly shit my pants. I stood in front of him and waited. I stood in silence for what felt like an eternity, but in reality, was only about twenty to thirty minutes. He looked at me and simply said, "I'm so disappointed in you." That was it. Nothing else. No punishment. Those five words nearly destroyed me.

It was then, right at this moment, I realised yes, I had got what I wanted—I was home, but at what cost? All I had ever wanted was my parents' approval. Their opinions mattered more than they probably should. I just wanted them to be proud of me, and I seemed to be continuously messing it up. While trying to find out where I fitted in the world, I felt like I was constantly disappointing them. I felt like I couldn't win.

CHAPTER FOUR

"WE RISE BY LIFTING OTHERS." — UNKNOWN.

When I was home from school during the school holidays, I would hang out with some of the older guys I'd met while at secondary school. Not the younger ones who'd taken my innocence. To me, the older boys were still my friends. In my mind, they wanted to see me, hang out with me. That meant they liked me. Right? It simply didn't matter what I was offering, platonic, sexual, it didn't matter. They were my friends and they wanted to see me.

I started to get a bit of a reputation at this point. Not a good one either. At the time, I honestly didn't think too much of it. It made me feel like I had made it, to be one of the "cool kids". Boys wanted to hang out with me, see me. That made me feel amazing. It never seemed to bother me that it was never any girls who wanted to be my friend. I just wanted friends, and to be fair, you could have been a fucking hedgehog and I'd have felt amazing about it. Jesus, I just wanted friends. Was that really so bad?

I soon caught on the girls in my town hated me. Because I was able to hook up with whatever guy I wanted. Not because I had a body to die for, not because I was beautiful, but because I gave them whatever they wanted. You ever seen the movie *DUFF*? I was the "duff". I wore clothes I had absolutely no business wearing, there wasn't a pound of flesh in the right place, but yet again, I didn't care. I was getting the attention. Not these other beautiful girls with figures I'd have frankly given my right tit for. Because of my "I don't give a fuck" attitude, it was more often than not confused with confidence.

I started having relationships. Like proper boyfriend stuff. I was on cloud nine to start with. My first abusive relationship was verbal. The first six months were beyond amazing. The guy was good looking and treated me like a queen. Gave me everything I could have ever dreamed of. But it wasn't *things* I wanted from him. My love language was and always will be touch. He'd hold my hand, play with my hair, stroke my back as we were falling asleep. He'd wear the aftershave I'd bought him for Christmas. To most, it would seem silly, immature even, but this was all I'd craved. When he told me he loved me? I thought I'd died and gone to Heaven.

Almost six months to the day our relationship started, he switched. It was almost as if he'd decided while eating his toast that morning, "that's it now, no more Mr. Nice Guy". Suddenly I became fat and ugly to him. He would tell me every day the only reason he was with me is because no one else would want me, and he felt sorry for me. Words which entangled themselves in deep seated feelings from years before. Words that cut so deep, I could almost see the blood dripping from the gash he just caused in my heart. At that point I knew he'd said these things because he'd had a bad day, or because something I'd done had annoyed him. I knew I was going to stay with him because I was going to do better. Be better. Be what he really wanted me to be. He didn't mean those ugly words. I was the ugly one and I was going to change.

But no matter what I did, what I changed, who I became and how hard I tried, he didn't change. I stayed because I loved him, and I knew there was good in him somewhere. But honestly, there was a much bigger reason I stayed. What if what he'd said was right? What if I was too ugly, too fat, to be worthy of love? Would I ever have this opportunity again? To be with someone who'd said he loved me. I was afraid, so very afraid of being alone.

When he finally left me, I was shattered. Physically, mentally, any way you can be broken, I was, and I didn't think I'd ever find the strength again to put myself back together. My best friend tried. God, she tried to help. But I found myself in a place I didn't want to be in, and there was no way I was dragging her down with me. So, I started to distance myself from people, push them away because if they weren't emotionally close to me, I couldn't hurt them with the apparently new toxic attitude I'd developed.

He started seeing someone new. Someone younger, prettier, and thinner. She was beautiful and everything I wasn't. I think I found that a really hard pill to swallow. So when he called, messaged, whatever, I always said yes. Random hook-ups because he wanted them. I was still in love with him. Infatuated, and everything in my life at that point was about him. How I could get him to spend time with me, speak to me. Anything. I know that made me sound like some desperate girl, but I didn't care. I cared about nothing else except him. He was my "be all and end all." Except he didn't feel the same. I was convenient for him—easy. I know what I was. But I didn't care. My self-worth had fallen so beyond low nothing mattered when it came to me. Literally nothing.

It was at this point my choices led me down a path I have no intention of ever going down again. I turned to drugs. Ones of the completely illegal variety and not my finest hour. All I really remember for about six months is a couple of flashes of a club and losing an awful lot of weight. That's it. And yet still, even having lost all this weight, I was still unhappy.

CHAPTER FIVE

"NOTHING IS PARTICULARLY HARD IF YOU BREAK IT DOWN INTO SMALL JOBS." — UNKNOWN.

I'd met my best friend at the beginning of the shitstorm of that first relationship. We'd gone to a local pub for a drink and a game of darts. She was working behind the bar that night. Turns out I'm terrible at maths. She took pity on me I think, as the boyfriend had started belittling me in front of everyone. That night, all I remember thinking of was what I could do to make this girl, this woman, my friend. She was amazing. Confident, comfortable around people, and funny. I didn't have any friends, I hadn't been allowed, but I wanted her as my friend. Like I said before though, I just needed to work out who I needed to be for her to like me.

I didn't see her that much after then unless we were in the pub. I remember thinking once maybe she actually liked me. Genuinely wanted to be my friend. I got called stupid for thinking that. He laughed in my face and told me I was an idiot for thinking someone might actually want to be my friend.

After about six months or so after that first relationship tanked, I met someone new. Someone I could laugh with, have a good time with. Someone who made me feel special. Wanted. Here I was again, in this place where I felt like I belonged. He didn't even wait to lull me into a false sense of security. The comments started pretty early on. "You're useless," "Why are you wearing that?"

"You look like a slut." Every single thing that went wrong became my fault somehow. He'd gaslight me at every opportunity. Then, he hit me. That time it was only once, and my knee-jerk reaction was to frantically apologise to him. He didn't mean it. I'd made him angry somehow. It was clearly my fault and the direct result of something I'd done. I remember begging him for forgiveness, promising to do better, be better.

I never seemed to be good enough. For anyone. I felt like I was always letting people down. I made a mental resolution then to change. Again. I would become this submissive doormat. Doing whatever it took to make the people in my life happy. Regardless of the consequences to me or my mental health.

But it was never quite good enough. I was never quite good enough. He continued to hit me. He'd never punch me. Ever. It was always an open-handed slap. And always across the face, or head if I flinched and moved. He did it this way because it never bruised. Not visibly. But shit, the guy worked with scaffolding and in construction, so he was strong and frankly, those slaps fucking hurt.

Chapter Six

"A GIRL SHOULD BE TWO THINGS: WHO AND WHAT SHE WANTS." — COCO CHANEL.

I eventually came clean to my best friend. She was my one constant. My one light in the very dark world I found myself in. I left the boyfriend with the strength of my best friend behind me. It did not go well, but I saw it through.

I had begun to realise maybe, just maybe, she saw something real in me. Something she liked about the person I was. It was honestly a strange, unfamiliar feeling for me. I'd never actually had a friend. Not someone who didn't want something from me. I had stopped taking anyone to my house. I still lived with my parents, and we lived in a beautiful, big house. The kind where you drive up to it and think "wow." My dad had worked incredibly hard for what he had, and he deserved the life him and Mum were living. I was just staying there until I could get my shit together long enough to get a life of my own. I didn't take people there, because simply, the moment we pulled up, you could literally see pound signs in their eyes. Then they'd start using me for money. Asking me to hang out, go to a club, go to the pub, whatever. But because of the desperate fucking need I had of wanting to be liked, I'd spend money on them. They'd invited me out, but all of a sudden, they didn't have money to cover anything. It was okay though because I always made sure I had enough.

I remember vividly, taking my best friend to my house for the first time. I don't really know why I did it. I think I was testing her. A really shitty thing to do in hindsight. But I needed to know. Was our friendship genuine, or was she the same as everyone else? The short answer is simply, no. She was different. But why? What was it in me she saw? Why in the hell did she like me? Enough to want to be my friend. I was terrified. Was she just biding her time until she got what she wanted? Was this new friendship going to suddenly come crashing down?

I didn't need to worry though. She stuck with me through all my ups and downs. All my insecurities, failed relationships. It may have looked like I had it all together. I didn't. Far from it. I wore a mask really bloody well. I still do a lot of the time, for new people I meet, people I don't know or trust.

Trust. I feel like that's a big word. I don't trust. I did back in the beginning. When my world was filled with rainbows and unicorn farts of glitter. Once I met you back then, I trusted you completely. Without fail and without question. I learned pretty fast though, trust gets you hurt. So I simply stopped trusting. I would let people get to know me on my terms. Never let them get too close. Show people what they want to see. The life and soul of the party. The girl who simply didn't give a fuck about anything or anyone. I was always up for anything, and it seemed to work because people wanted me around. People wanted to hang out with me and be a part of my "I don't care" life.

But I did care. And I was miserable. I hated my life. I hated myself. I hated what I had become just so I could feel wanted and like I had friends. I would go home after a night out and cry. I'd sob for hours in the safety of my bedroom. My parents had no clue; I hid it from them very well because I simply didn't want them to know how low I had fallen. I don't know if they will ever read this. It doesn't matter if they do. This is my story, my life, and more importantly, my truth.

CHAPTER SEVEN

"WHAT YOU DO TODAY CAN IMPROVE ALL YOUR TOMORROWS." — RALPH MARSTON.

I had a few meaningless relationships if I can even call them that. But I'd get dumped pretty quickly because I'd come off as needy, clingy. Each time I got dumped, another little bit of my heart got chipped away and I instantly reverted back to the fat kid in school who was never good enough. Why though? Why was I never fucking good enough? I never felt like I was good enough to have friends, to have a boyfriend who actually wanted to be with me for me. I was a good person. I gave everyone what they wanted, regardless of what that may have been, a lift somewhere, money, something sexual, anything. But I learned later in life people will just use you unless you learn the word "no," to stay true to yourself. It's only then you find your true friends, the people who genuinely want to be around.

I decided there and then I think I was simply destined to be less than. It wasn't what I'd wanted out of life, but it was clearly what He had decided for me. I lived my life without dreams, without hopes for any accomplishments. Nothing. I was nothing. As sad as it may sound, it's how I genuinely felt about myself.

The next couple of years were spent drinking and making bad choices. My friend and I would go out nearly every night to our local town. They had a couple of pubs/clubs, one in particular we had frequented so often we knew the owners and all the doormen/bouncers. But more importantly, being a military town, there were soldiers. Lots and lots of soldiers. Easy on the eye boys that were always looking for one thing.

Having spent so much time with my friend, I realised she was in a way, the same as me. She put on a mask as well. For reasons I won't go into here. Not my story to tell. But we'd go out, adorn our masks, and become literally the life and soul of the party. Suddenly, without even realising it, I had what I'd always wanted. People. People who liked me, people who wanted to be around me. People who would get excited I'd walked into the bar. I still don't know why they liked me or if they actually did. I didn't care though. When I went out, I became a different person to the one I was when I was at home. I was living two different lives and I honestly didn't know which alter ego I preferred at that point.

With this new, very fake confidence, I could get what I wanted, who I wanted. It didn't matter to me that these relationships, platonic or romantic, were built on lies. Lies of my own making, a fake platform I'd built to please people. Because here we go again, always falling back to the normal I knew of just wanting to be liked, to have friends. I hated myself, and I knew in order for people to like me, I had to be someone I'm not naturally.

My friend and I became verbally aggressive. Making fun of people, sarcasm always there in conversations. Belittling people without them even realising. I projected my inner hurt, my inner destruction onto those that were around me.

CHAPTER EIGHT

"IT ALWAYS SEEMS IMPOSSIBLE UNTIL IT'S DONE." — NELSON MANDELA.

The boy I was seeing at that particular time had gone away on some military training exercise. I went out, my friend and I met up with a group of guys in the club. There was flirting, the usual sarcasm, but it had turned out to be a pretty good night. The guy I had been talking to, let's call him "shithead", had a conversation with me that night about my boyfriend. I was very upfront with him, I wasn't available. I remember him asking me what my definition of cheating was. But I'm loyal, still am loyal to a fault. If I was with a boy, no matter about the condition of the relationship, I was fucking loyal. Regardless. Channing Tatum could have walked in and declared his undying love to me, I'd have sighed, inwardly cursed myself, and declined his advances. Probably sarcastically.

That night, May 21st, 2001, my world flipped on its axis, again. This guy had seemed to take the hint when I'd told him that I wasn't single, I drove him back to camp, via the kebab house. He asked if we could sit a minute and finish our food. It was something I had no problem with because the guys I'd done it with before knew I was closed off, and they found me intimidating to the point they knew not to fuck with me. I was everybody's friend, until you crossed me. Easy.

I had learned how to completely disassociate from my feelings. If I didn't have any, then I couldn't get hurt. Right? No, very, very wrong.

He tried that night. God, did he try. He tried to shove his hand down my jeans and into my knickers, he tried to shove his hand up into my t-shirt when he worked out going south wasn't going to work. I remember him telling me "I will fucking have you, everyone else has." But the funny thing? It wasn't true. Yes, I'd done things I wasn't proud of, most things other than full intercourse, but boys will talk. And they'd rather spin a lie or a version of the truth because squaddies (soldiers) had a reputation to protect. Couldn't let it be known they'd gone out, got together with a girl, and then hadn't actually sealed the deal.

I was too tired to argue the point. I didn't care. Not on the outside anyway. Deep down, far away from anywhere anyone could actually see, I craved acceptance. Love. I thought the way I was going about it, was going to help me find my forever. What I did find was far from what I wanted. I found pain, loneliness. I found that my inability to trust sunk deeper and deeper into some imaginary abyss inside my head.

Anyway, I bit the guy. Hard enough I could taste his blood in my mouth. It didn't taste metallic like blood normally would – I'm not actually a vampire, but when you get nose bleeds etc – it tasted sweet. I vividly remember smiling and he saw. He called me a sadistic bitch and promised me he would "finish the job properly" the following night. I think he knew it was a given that I go out both nights of the weekend.

Joke was on him though. I didn't go out the following night. Well, I tried not to. My friend called me and asked where I was. I explained I wasn't coming out that night because I didn't have any money. Anyone who knew me back then would know, without question, that was an absolute out and out lie. I would go out whether I had money or not. I never needed to pay a door charge to get into the club, and I made a glass of Coke last all night, if I even bought it at all. She asked me what was wrong, what was the real reason for my absence? I gave her the Cliff Notes and explained that while I was more than capable of looking after myself, I simply didn't have the energy for it. She seemed to accept my sorry excuse.

Except she didn't. After I hung up with her, I settled back into the sofa and started watching whatever crap was on the TV that night. I wasn't really watching it at this point though. I was wondering if this guy had made good his threat and gone to the club that night looking for me. Wasn't that what I'd wanted for most of my life? Someone "looking" for me? Yeah, but shit not like this. The saying "be careful what you wish for" seemed all too relevant then.

My phone rang again. Fuck it, why can't people just leave me alone? It was one of the doormen from the club. I knew them all. I liked them all and I genuinely felt they looked out for me when the bad choices I'd make came into play. He told me he'd spoken to my friend and him and the other doormen believed the guy was there. I asked him how he could possibly know that. He told me someone loosely fitting the description was in the club and constantly looking at the door. As if waiting for someone. He asked me if I'd be happy to come in to tell them if it was the guy or not. Fuck no I wouldn't. He simply told me it was tough because he was already sitting in my driveway waiting to take me there. He explained they wanted him identified so they could get the police involved. That didn't work out for me so well when I was sixteen, why the hell would it work out now?

I went with him anyway. I knew I was safe with him and he would never in a million years let anything bad happen to me. We got to the club, the bouncers explained where he was and then flanked me. Two in front, two behind, and the one who'd come to get me holding my hand next to me. As I looked out into the room, through the fire doors I saw a mass of people. It was almost a scene of Biblical proportions. Everyone else became blurred except this one guy. If anyone else had been in my head then, looking through my eyes, it would have been a scene from some kind of messed up comedy show. As I looked at him and our eyes met, two things happened simultaneously. I jerked forward to rip his throat out and he made a surprisingly quick escape for the fire exit. Funny thing though, the fire exit was locked. Always was. I had the bouncer next to me and the ones behind me restraining me, as the two from the front made a dash for him. The next second as I looked up, this guy, who seemed so strong and manly the night before, was now face first on the floor, kicking, screaming, and crying. Crying.

CHAPTER NINE

"EACH TIME A WOMAN STANDS UP FOR HERSELF, SHE STANDS UP FOR ALL WOMEN." —MAYA ANGELOU.

The police were called, statements given in the room downstairs to the main club. The room was small and badly lit. There were two chairs, which looked like they might be comfortable, but they were old and the padding on the seat was more like sitting on concrete and they scraped across the concrete floor when you moved them. A noise that would normally set anyone's ears on edge, but I found it comforting. It matched the noise in my head and gave me a warped sense of peace. My bouncer friend sat on the other chair and had his hand on my knee. I knew he wanted to give me support and let me know he was there for me, but I hated supportive touch. The "It's okay, we're here for you," kind of touch. I never felt liked I deserved it, so I typically recoiled from it. The two police officers who had come down with us, were forced to stand in what was left of this tiny room. I didn't hear anything for a couple of weeks until one afternoon I got a call from an unknown number. I was just getting out of my car when I answered. I'm glad now I had already parked. If I'd still been driving, when the person on the other end of the phone told me no further action was being taken, I probably would've driven straight into a tree. The person told me because the shithead said that yes, there had been an encounter, but I was consensual, there wasn't really anything they could do. I asked what about the bite mark? They explained he'd simply said I was kinky. I liked it rough. I wasn't, and I didn't. Remember earlier when I said my love language was touch? Yeah, that. I was absolutely not into any kind of sadism or rape kink.

So that was that. Yet again, my life was spun around, and I frankly didn't know my arse from my elbow at that point. I started to drink. Heavily. I simply didn't care anymore. I remember my friend sitting me down one day when I had just finished work, ergo, I was sober, and asking me to stop. Stop the drinking, stop the reckless behaviour. Just be me again. But I didn't know who "me" was. I don't think I had ever really known who me was. I would like to think she had started to drift away from me at that point. Filling my head with thoughts that she simply couldn't watch her friend go through that. Watching me put myself through that. But in reality, however hard this pill is to swallow, it was the other way round. I started pulling away from her. From everyone. I completely lost myself in the turmoil in my head. If I didn't have anyone close, then I couldn't get hurt or hurt anyone. It was easier that way. The choices I made from then on seemed to be the easy choices to make. But they weren't. They were hard because I had no one. I was on my own, completely of my own making and it hurt.

I started doing stupid things. Dangerous things. My sudden need for adrenalin almost consumed me and I would get out of my mind drunk, and decided playing chicken with cars and lorries, jumping out of the way at the last minute, would be a good idea. I never cared about the impact it might have had on the driver had I not moved. I would pick fights with people, for absolutely no fucking reason at all. Hoping they'd beat the shit out of me badly enough I'd either die or have some sort of life altering damage. That never happened either. I didn't care and I decided the world would be a much better place without me in it. I may have been right, but it was clear I was a fuck up at trying to fuck it all up. Ironic how that happens.

CHAPTER TEN

"I CAN AND I WILL, WATCH ME." — UNKNOWN.

My world came to a head when I was sitting in the middle of a random high street somewhere in Hampshire. I started hearing laughter. Proper belly laughing and I couldn't for the life of me find a source. But then I did. I had spent about ten minutes looking around, slowly at first, then rapidly getting faster and faster. Almost frantic, trying to find the owner of this laughing sound.

Then I found it. But to my absolute horror, the sound belonged to a man who must have been over six foot tall. Wearing, would you believe, a bright pink tutu and leotard, ballet shoes in a weird beige colour and a tiara. It was at this exact point, I knew I had a problem. A big problem, but I couldn't work out how I could help myself, so I called my doctor. Well, I called the health centre where my doctor worked and insisted I needed an appointment at the earliest opportunity. They asked why and I think I told them I was losing my mind. I thought I was literally seeing things. She got me in for an appointment the next day. I remember thinking I just had to push through. No matter how scared I was, I had to get through whatever the hell this was until I could see my doctor.

I didn't sleep that night. I was so incredibly scared about what was happening to me. I didn't understand and I certainly couldn't wrap my head around what could possibly be going on. I lay in bed paralysed with pure fear. I had never been this scared. When people are doing things to you, there's a part of your brain that understands that it is happening to you, you aren't choosing this life. But when you're faced with things like hallucinations, that is something you don't have any control over. Not only is it not someone doing something to you, but your brain, your mind, seem to be messing with you as well. So your own mental health has taken away your control as well. The one thing I'd always had was my own control. Apparently not anymore.

I got to my appointment about twenty minutes early and just sat in the car park. I've always been a stickler for timekeeping, being late for anything makes me seriously anxious, so I try to be early for every appointment, every meeting.

I went into that appointment not knowing what to expect, but I knew I had to be truthful, honest, about how I was really feeling and what had happened the day before. The doctor, a middle-aged, blonde woman, looked at me with sympathetic eyes and said, "I think we need to get you some help."

She picked up her telephone and dialled a number. I don't remember the conversation or even if I actually heard it. I was suddenly transported, in my head, to a different place. Somewhere happier, somewhere softer. When she put the phone down, she'd apparently had to say my name several times for me to mentally come back into the room with her, she explained she'd made me an appointment with an emergency psychiatrist at a mental health facility and I was to go up there immediately, they were expecting me.

I had absolutely no idea what I was walking in to. I arrived at the hospital, in somewhat of a daze. I probably shouldn't have driven there myself; I honestly couldn't even tell you if I did drive myself or if someone drove me. I have no memory of actually arriving there at all. I know the unit I had to report to wasn't on the first floor, but again, I have no recollection of getting upstairs.

I do, however, remember getting to the actual unit. Walking up to what appeared to be the most imposing door I'd ever seen. Brown, it was your typical NHS brown with safety glass routinely slotted between further slabs of brown wood. The walls were the nastiest beige/brown colour and reminded me of vomit. I remember smirking at the thought. I guess it was my way of coping in a situation I had zero control over. I had no idea what was about to happen and the events that were about to unfold.

I pressed a buzzer as I'd already tried the door and it wouldn't budge. I explained who I was and why I was there and heard an echoing click. The door had been released and I was met by the friendly face of a nurse who asked me to follow her.

I was taken to a room that was, at best, bland. Again, a nasty beige colour for the walls, no pictures or flowers, a desk and two chairs. There wasn't a computer or anything that would give a person any hint as to what happened in this room. It's kind of amusing the things you remember when you're facing a life-changing event. For me, it's typically the sounds or smells, colours or lack-thereof.

In walks a man, all I remember was that he was shorter than me and a lot older. I think he was Indian, although I can't really remember. I can quite happily tell you he had on stripy suit trousers and very scuffed black shoes. I couldn't tell you what we talked about, but I know he knew about my hallucinations and my current state of mental health. He suggested I be admitted to the mental health unit, and I went into a tail spin. I had heard some of other "patients", I hadn't had the pleasure of seeing any yet but there was no way in Hell I was going to be staying there, not even for one night.

I asked the doctor if I could call my parents to come and get me, he eventually agreed, but only on the promise I wasn't going to hurt myself or anyone else. I'd honestly have promised to fly to the moon as long as it meant I didn't have to stay in this shit hole for longer than absolutely necessary.

I went and sat in the main lounge once I'd called my mum. There was a woman in there rocking. She realised I may not be sticking around and asked if I could go to the shop for her since I was leaving. Me, being blissfully naïve said sure. I asked her what she wanted, "Vodka". One word. Yeah, sorry but no. I had never felt more out of place than I did sitting in that room. I have no idea how long it took for my parents to arrive, but it felt like an eternity.

Suddenly, I felt a gentle tap on my shoulder, whispered words of "Emma, your mum is here," and I was quickly ushered out to the waiting arms of Mum.

I've never been more grateful to see her. She wrapped her arms around me, tighter than she ever has before and said, "Let's go home, Daddy is waiting." We got down to the car where I could see my dad sitting in the driver's seat. Mum had briefly explained he couldn't handle going up to get me. I didn't understand at the time, but I did brush it off and just relished in the fact he'd even come to get me.

"Stay positive, work hard, make it happen." – Unknown.

My friend basically told me to get my shit together. I was worth more than this. My life was worth more than this. Normally I would have told her to fuck off. But when I looked her in the eye, at her command, I saw something that shook me to my core. Sounds really poetic, but I saw tears. I didn't know if they were for me, or if she'd got something in her eye, but they were there. She saw me, the real, vulnerable, and sad me. She told me she'd stood back and watched as I tried to throw my life away for long enough and she wasn't going to stand back anymore. Now, here's the thing, I can be intimidating, but back then, my friend really was intimidating, even to me sometimes. Rarely, but sometimes. I must have sat back and paid attention, because from then on, I started to get some semblance of my life back together. I stopped drinking, completely. I'll pour myself a glass of wine at Christmas, but I won't drink it. Other than that, I don't drink at all now.

Life didn't just turn around for me. It was hard work. I still didn't like myself very much and genuinely believed people just wanted to be friends with me to see what they could get from me. I didn't trust. At all. Again, easier that way. My relationship with my mum had started to improve, because up until that point, I'd almost ruined it completely. I was fairly sure I'd hurt her. Actually, hurt doesn't quite cover it to be honest. I'd been everything you didn't want a daughter to be. It was a fucking miracle she was still talking to me at all.

By this point, and a decent number of miracles, I'd made it to twenty-five. I'm still not sure how I made it that far. I'd made stupid choices. But I'd also had a lot of laughs. The dark was always there. Always. But every now and again, I had moments of pure clarity. Pure joy. I didn't think I'd have made it this far if it hadn't been for my Faith. My belief in God had never wavered. I knew He had a purpose for me. I had no damn clue what that purpose was. What form it took, how it would be delivered to me, no idea at all. But I held onto the belief it was there none-the-less. It had to be. I was holding on to it like my life almost depended on it. I guess it did to a point.

"She was powerful not because she wasn't scared but because she went on so strongly, despite the fear." – Atticus.

I met Robert in the second week of October in 2002. It was actually, still is, a pretty amusing story. I was visiting a friend in her flat. Her boyfriend and her daughter were there, along with another girlfriend. The boyfriend got a phone call and all I heard was the backend of his conversation, saying "I'll see you in a minute then". My friend asked who he had been speaking to and once he'd explained it was "Robert" all Hell broke loose. The girl who was visiting with me started running around getting changed, putting on some make-up etc, trying to make herself somewhat decent. Girl code and all that, it was clear, even to the blind, she fancied him, so there was no way in Hell I was even going to so much as glance at him. Honestly, I was fine with that. I had just got out of yet another emotionally abusive relationship and my confidence was visiting with the Diablo anyway. When you see yourself as the back end of a dead cow, how can you expect anyone else to find you even remotely attractive? So I was more than happy to sit back, drink my coffee and watch the shit show that was inevitably about to happen.

Well, bugger me stupid. That shit show happened in a way I never thought possible. In walks this man. Not a boy. A man. And I knew, somehow, at some point in time, I was going to marry him. It confused the piss out of me. He was literally the complete opposite of anyone I'd hooked up with prior. He was older than me, balding, back and chest hair (gross – but I secretly love it now). I didn't understand what I was feeling, but I figured I'd just go with it.

That day we talked for a good while. About three hours we sat on the stairs of my friend's flat just talking. About everything and nothing. Nothing important, but everything that mattered that day. I still don't understand it, but that day, I suddenly felt more at peace than I'd ever felt. I was home. Not literally, I was sitting on a set of shitty stairs, but in my heart. My soul. I knew I was home.

"Strong women don't play the victim. Don't make themselves look pitiful and don't point fingers. They stand and they deal." – Mandy Hale.

I think that it is at this point the shit really hit the fan. All of a sudden, my heart knew love. Acceptance. I had absolutely no idea what to do with that. Did I deserve to be happy? Did I deserve to feel these butterflies? In my mind, no. It was as simple as that.

All this time, all the self-destruction and self-sabotage led me to this one point. I realised, very suddenly, I'd never believed in suicide. At the back of my mind, all I was thinking was God had some bigger purpose for me. That somehow, He would see me through everything I was doing to myself. I'd never self-harmed but thoughts of "un-aliving" had crossed my mind, but never really for any decent amount of time, and never really seriously. They were just thoughts. I think honestly, I'm simply too much of a coward to take my own life. I could never do that to the people I loved. It was never about how they felt about me, it was all about how I felt about them. My parents, my brother, my best friend. I loved them. They were my everything and I simply didn't want to leave them. Funny, isn't it? One can look back on those times and recognise how hard they were, and then rationalise them and everything just slots into place.

All this time, through all the pain, the heartache, and the confusion, I'd existed. One painful, exhausting day just rolled into another. Someone once asked me how I got through it. Honestly, I don't know. I really don't. I think I just held on to the hope it has to get better, easier at some point? It just had to. But because I didn't believe in suicide, I didn't have a choice but to hold on, with everything I had.

Don't get me wrong, my life hasn't been shit every single day. The negative thoughts have pretty much always been there, but I've laughed. I've found ways to find the good in people, to find the good in situations and laugh.

Meeting Robert changed everything for me. And the change happened fast. Take me by surprise fast.

I don't know what triggered this episode. I actually have very little memory of that day at all. I think it was a combination of things, from all of the unhappiness

I'd dealt with to that point, to the sudden feelings of happiness I felt at meeting this man, completely out of nowhere.

I knew I'd gone up to the cemetery to sit with my friend. He'd died several years before, and I often found solace sitting with him. Just chatting. Like going to confession without the priest part. It was my safe place if you will.

I don't remember how long I was there for, or what I even talked to him about. The first thing I remember thinking was I hoped this spitting coming from the sky doesn't turn into rain. It was weird though. Because I felt constant "drops" landing on my ankle, but I couldn't see any rain. That's when I looked down at my ankle and saw, not water, but blood. I'd cut. For the first time in my life, I'd hurt myself, and honestly, it scared the absolute piss out of me. It was at this point I knew I'd hit a level so low, for me, I was going to go one of two ways. I could either get the help I clearly needed or ignore it. Like I had done so many times in the past. Push the pain away, and it won't hurt anymore.

I needed help. I chose help. I went to the one place where I'd felt even remotely safe, happy, it was also the closest to me, geographically. I don't know how I got there; I can only assume I drove. I got to my friend's house and somehow, she immediately knew what to do. I sat up on her kitchen counter and I'll never forget what she asked me. She asked a couple of standard questions, but the one that got to me, even still to this day it gives me chills, was "are you safe around my daughter?" My answer was no, I'm not. That was a hard pill to swallow but I knew I'd done the right thing by choosing to help and not hide.

She tried to help; her partner tried to help. But in reality, there was only one person I wanted anywhere near me. Robert. A phone call was made, and a flurry of activity happened. I don't know what. He arrived, my knight in shining armour. I know it sounds really cheesy, but it was my reality.

We left the house and he took the reins from there. He patched up my arm, cleaned me up and encouraged me to talk. Not the superficial kind of talking. He encouraged me to start talking about the hard stuff. The stuff from my childhood. From my teens and early adulthood. We talked, well I did, for about five hours. He just sat and listened as I poured my heart and soul out to him.

Something happened to me then. I felt lighter than I have ever felt. I know it sounds clichéd, but I'd never been encouraged to talk before, really talk.

CHAPTER ELEVEN

"ENERGY IS TRANSFERABLE, SO BE CAREFUL OF THE COMPANY YOU KEEP. DIRT WILL RUB OFF ON WHITE, BEFORE WHITE RUBS OFF ON DIRT." — UNKNOWN.

It was at this moment, when I'd laid myself bare, I realised something monumental. I was strong. Mentally. I always had been. But I'd never had the opportunity to embrace it and understand it. Not truly. It was my "light bulb" moment. I'd seen them happen in movies, read about them in books, and always almost scoffed at the ridiculousness of them. That shit doesn't happen in real life. But it did and it was happening to me.

After my soul-baring moment with Robert, I decided to have some time to myself. Finding my inner badass and trying to formulate a plan on how I was going to proceed from here. It wasn't as easy as I'd hoped it was going to be. I didn't wake up the next morning with some new personality. I knew it was going to take hard work, and a lot of this newfound strength.

If you've got this far in my shit show, then you have that same strength, or you want it. And that's half your battle won. You want to be better. You don't want to be a shadow of who you can really be.

I decided the strength I've always had was going to come up to the forefront.

CHAPTER TWELVE

"YOU CAN'T GO BACK AND CHANGE THE BEGINNING, BUT YOU CAN START WHERE YOU ARE AND CHANGE THE ENDING." — C.S. LEWIS.

Robert and I talked, a lot. We laughed, cried, and talked some more. I told him I couldn't have children. At some point in my early twenties, I'd been diagnosed with something called Scheuermann's disease. I had pain in my back. Sometimes a lot, sometimes not so much. This disease I was told I had typically hit adolescents and mostly boys. When I was diagnosed, I was neither an adolescent nor a boy. I was a medical mystery. I was also told my spine simply wasn't strong enough to carry a child, so it would be unwise of me to get pregnant.

I remember when I was initially told, it didn't bother me. I was in my early twenties; I didn't want kids anyway. But now? Now I'd met this incredible man, and although it was far too early to talk about kids with Robert, I started to think maybe I did want them. It certainly got me thinking.

CHAPTER THIRTEEN

"THE WORLD BREAKS EVERYONE, AND AFTERWARD, MANY ARE STRONG AT THE BROKEN PLACES." — ERNEST HEMINGWAY.

In January 2003, Robert asked me to marry him. January 26th, to be exact. I had honestly never known happiness like it. Finally, finally I had what I'd only ever dared dream about. I had the fairy tale and my world suddenly slotted into place.

We'd always agreed to take it slowly. We'd both been in pretty traumatic relationships prior to getting together and didn't want to rush anything. But, when you know, you know.

We were friends first. That was really important to us. I had told him about my past very early on. I still don't know why I did . I trusted him right from the start after my breakdown. I think I figured if he was going to run, then hearing about my past would be the thing to make him run. I think I saw it as I was giving him a "get out" clause right at the beginning. He didn't run. It was then we decided to first become friends, before anything physical happened.

When we'd first gotten together, I remember he'd asked me to go for a drink. He was working this particular night in the Rugby Club. He was a serving soldier and his whole life revolved around the military.

I'd explained I didn't have any money for a drink (shocker), and he'd told me it was fine. He'd buy me a couple of drinks. Joke was on him though because I could put away a lot of alcohol back then. I went down there with the friends who'd introduced me to Robert in the first place.

That night was an amazing night and one I remember with incredible clarity. When he was on a break (which was pretty often) we sat and chatted. Poor guy made the mistake of assuming we were now dating. I told him it was rude to assume and if he wanted to date me, he had to ask me properly. So he rolled his eyes, smirked, and asked me to be his girlfriend. I sat quietly, pretending to be deep in thought and said, "Yeah, why not." He grinned from ear to ear and leaned in for a kiss.

I instantly freaked out—or so he thought—and asked him what the hell he thought he was doing? I then told him he had to ask for permission to kiss me. Inside I was dying laughing, as were my friends, but he thought I was dead serious. He'll tell you now, he knew I was messing around, but he didn't, not really. He did ask though.

That set the tone for our relationship. On the outside, I was happy-go-lucky, the class clown. We laughed, we had fun, we became the best of friends. We spent all our time together. That was until he got shipped out to Iraq in the May of 2003. Weird, isn't it? How the love of my life is fighting in some war I knew very little about, and suddenly through the letters we were writing to each other, my walls were cracking. Crumbling down with each and every single word I wrote to him. Slowly but surely, I was showing him my vulnerabilities. My broken.

But he still didn't run. He didn't tell me I was too much. Instead, he held me when he got home and told me he loved me. He loved me and he couldn't wait to marry me. But I was terrified. All my old, deep-seated worries started to seep in. What if I wasn't enough for him. Not pretty enough, not funny enough, not clever enough? All the insecurities I'd ever felt were trying desperately to get through my shell.

But I wasn't going to let them win. I had found an amazing man, told him about my past (I hate secrets – they don't sit well with me, never have) and my fears, he'd heard it all from me and he hadn't flinched. He had told me he loved me regardless. So I went with it. I accepted he was telling me the truth and that he wasn't like the rest. I gave him the benefit of the doubt and just trusted what he was telling me. I'd done that in the past and been burned, but I believed in fairy tales. Romance and love. So, I believed this was the real deal, and if it turned out not to be, then I'd deal with that if and when it happened.

On December 19th, 2003, I said "I do" to my best friend. I wore the most amazing off-white dress, with crystals all over the top of the bodice, they fell down the left side of the dress all the way down the skirt portion and were stitched all around the back of the dress and into the train. My veil had little crystals dotted around throughout and sat on top of my head with a beautiful diamond tiara. My mum had worn the same tiara at her wedding, and it had belonged to my grandpa's side of the family. It was one of those super fancy pieces that lived in a vault for most of its life. Being pulled out for special occasions. It absolutely made me feel like a princess and suddenly I was living out my real-life fairy tale.

I remember walking up the aisle to my forever. The man who accepted me absolutely as I was. He never judged, never made me feel less-than. Just loved me for me.

And then it hit me like a freight train. I wasn't suddenly happy *because* of him. I was happy because of *me*. The hell I'd been through had bought me to this point. I saw my past as a series of pebbled roads, and they all led me to where I was right now. I'm a huge believer in Fate. I genuinely believed I went through the pain and heartache so I could fully appreciate what I was getting ready to do.

Life got normal. Well, as normal as it could with a serving soldier. We became a unit. Slipped into married life like water flows through a river. I'm not normally that kind of poetic, suffice to say, we fit together. I'd found "my person". Of that I was 100% sure.

We did all the normal things couples do. Went out, meals, the bar on the military base, made friends. Friends. People who actually got me and I genuinely believed, people who liked me and my quirky personality. A lot of the guys we were friends with had gone to Iraq with Robert. The guys all had a common denominator that drew them together and the wives all had the same. We all became a group of people with a mutual respect for each other.

Chapter Fourteen

"Be powerful." — Perry Power.

In 2004, Robert got a posting in another area, so we packed up our house and moved. Moving was something I knew I'd have to become accustomed to. Little did I know, I was really going to get used to it.

Life became my version of "normal". Apparently my dad had always said I'd come good somewhere between the ages of twenty-six to fifty. A pretty broad range, but at least it gave me hope.

I learned how to accept happiness. Normalcy. The choices I had made in life up until this point, had led me to this point. I felt sure about that. We settled into a routine of him looking after me, and me learning how to be me. The true me. Without a mask on. I was genuinely happy, but in the same breath, I was always wondering if it would suddenly come crashing down around my feet. Did I deserve this? Every time I got a text from him, or when I'd see his name pop up on my phone, or even when I'd see him walking towards me when I hadn't seen him for the day, I'd get these stupid butterflies swirling around deep in my tummy. That still hasn't changed. My world became this man.

When we'd moved, I had to change my doctor. Catchment area and all that good stuff. I started seeing a new doctor and she questioned me about my medical history and most predominantly about my back. Robert and I had spoken about children and whether or not we wanted them. We had decided no. He already had children from a previous relationship, and I had been told I couldn't have them.

My new doctor asked me to do all sorts of different exercises and asked me various questions. I remember asking her what she was doing, why all the questions? She very simply told me that she didn't think I had this degenerative spinal disease. I explained I'd had a skiing accident years prior. It turns out I'd torn a load of muscles which hadn't repaired properly. Bring on six months of very intensive physiotherapy, and although my back still caused me some problems, it was nothing compared to what it had been. All of a sudden, my doctor tells me being pregnant wouldn't be a problem.

I sat down with Robert and explained what had been said, and then dropped the biggest bombshell of my life. I wanted children. Regardless of what had been said to me all those years ago, I knew in my soul I wanted children. I didn't care how many. Even if it was just one. He wasn't ready. He needed to think about it. You see, my husband had been married before and the marriage broke down pretty much straight after the child arrived. He was scared. I knew that, but I couldn't get this over riding feeling out of my heart. I knew I had to talk him round somehow, that having a baby with me was a good idea, it was something we both wanted.

We went to Germany in 2006 to visit with some of our friends, while we were out one night, Robert told me he thought he might be ready and we could start trying to get pregnant. I couldn't believe it. I was over the moon happy, and I spent the rest of the trip making sure he was sure. That he wasn't going to change his mind suddenly.

On the weekend after my birthday in September, my mum told me to take a pregnancy test, I spoke with Robert and he agreed. I took the test and I couldn't believe what I was seeing. Two little lines appeared on the pee stick. All of a sudden, I knew my world was going to change. I was beyond happy, terrified, and apprehensive. What a whirlwind of emotions.

I had an absolutely text book pregnancy. No morning sickness, no sleep deprivation, a few food or drink cravings, but everything went exactly as it should have. Baby was growing beautifully, and Robert and I couldn't have been happier. I flew back to the Middle East, where we were living at the time and did the majority of my pregnancy there. British Airways won't let you fly when you're thirty-four weeks or more pregnant. I turned thirty-four weeks the day I landed back in the UK. The guy who had been lucky enough to sit next to me on the plane, genuinely thought I was going to give birth at any moment. He helped me get off the plane, grab my bags, and then saw me through the arrivals section and safely handed me over to my parents who were waiting for me. Mum said the guy looked terrified and his face was white as a sheet.

I stayed in the UK to give birth, a very deliberate choice. Robert arrived a week before my due date, and sure enough, with a little medical help, our beautiful son arrived at 8:13 on Wednesday morning, May 9th. Eight pounds and thirteen ounces I don't ever say I gave birth. He was "created". He was so long. I'd bought loads of baby clothes, as you do, and hardly any of them fit him.

I mentioned a little medical help. It was actually considerably more than that. I had been in the "pushing" stage of labour for longer than I should have been. I had been assigned two midwives, one who had qualified a few months before, and one who was still training. My pregnancy had been so simple, why would the delivery not be any different? Joke was on me, or them, I can't work out which. Turns out my son was stuck, inside me. Shift change happened the morning after my contractions had started and a senior midwife came in, took one look "down south" and ran. I was high as a kite on the gas and air stuff they give you, so as she was running out all I saw were trails of colour following her as she left the room. Next thing I knew, a bald dude came rushing in, had a quick look and I was wheeled out of the delivery suite and rushed into theatre. I was being prepped for an emergency c-section. Apparently they decided to give it one last go with a natural birth, but it was going to have to be assisted.

I had a spinal block done, which ultimately left a bruise the size of a small planet on my spine, and the games began.

The doctor got my bundle of joy out with forceps. I had torn pretty badly anyway, but apparently I'd torn in the wrong place. I had to be cut. Between being cut, the delivery, and whatever the hell else happened, I managed to lose just shy of a pint of blood. I was ultimately sewn up, and sent back to the ward with my new baby. I was terrified. I had no idea what I was doing, and the nurses just kept telling me I needed to feed my son. I was trying. Like really trying, but the little bugger would not latch on to me. It turned out that he'd been damaged during the birthing process. The doctor had used too much force, too low down on his face with the forceps. He damaged some of the cranial muscles at the base of his skull and also the connecting part of my son's jaw. So he couldn't physically latch on to me. He's got a little dimple just below his cheek bone where the bone was damaged, he'll have it for the rest of his life.

I tried, nurses tried, a doctor tried. We had to feed him with these tiny little bottles just to get food in him. I'd had him on the Wednesday morning and my parents came up to see me in the evening. My mother, ever the tactful one, pulled a face. When I asked her what was wrong, she simply asked what the smell was. I had no clue what she was talking about and then it hit me like a freight train. It was me. I was the smell. It suddenly dawned on me I literally hadn't left my bed since I'd had the spinal block. I still had my catheter, a pad to stop any unwanted bleeding, and the sheets I'd given birth on. I don't know who was angrier at this point. My mum or my dad.

Suddenly, a flurry of activity happened around my bed. The curtain was closed, visitors, including my husband, were told to step aside. I had the catheter removed and was unceremoniously told to get up. I hadn't used my legs all day, so they were literal noodles. I put my first leg down and felt it wobble, when the next one followed, the nurse had to rush to my side until I could find the strength in my legs to actually stand up properly.

Robert then came in and was instructed to take me for a shower. He was told not to leave me alone, but to be careful of the lady garden area. I'd had stitches. By the time I'd come back to the bed, the sheets had been stripped and fresh ones were in their place. My parents were cuddling with our son and had the looks on their faces that can only be described as some kind of euphoria. First time grandparents and they clearly couldn't have been happier.

I was discharged from hospital the following lunchtime. I was a little shocked as I hadn't even got close to mastering breast feeding. It was something I desperately wanted to do. So I persevered.

By Friday morning, I was in agony. It's a pain I still struggle to describe efficiently. I had a midwife coming to see me anyway that morning so I asked her to take a look. She was appalled at what she saw. She explained my stitch, singular, had broken down. It was gone. She then told me, with a look of shame on her face, I should have had in excess of eighty-five individual stitches. Eighty-five.

I was told I was going to be given an emergency appointment with some gynaecologist. Top of his field I was told. He took one look at me and said there was nothing more he could do. No point re-stitching me as I would heal.

During the next three weeks, Robert had to shower me. I wasn't able to have a bath and I wasn't flexible enough to get to the hard to reach spots. I cried every shower time. Every time I went to the toilet, I had to shower. It was a nightmare along with a newborn, who still wasn't latching onto me properly.

My mum asked if maybe I wanted some help. She'd found a woman who was a breast feeding consultant. I had no idea what that even was, but I was willing to give anything a try. I was moving back to Saudi the following week with my new baby, Robert had already gone back, so I had to do something. This woman arrived, a little younger than Mum was, conservatively dressed and very "proper".

We went through some different exercises and actually found one that worked. I was naked from the waist up, my son was put on my belly and then he crawled his way up to the good stuff. He latched, almost immediately and began a delicious three course meal, courtesy of my boob. What no one had accounted for was the fact that my toes had almost curled in on themselves and I had tears pouring from my eyes. None of that was because it was a beautiful experience. I was feeling a pain that I had never felt before, it was beyond excruciating. Because of all the countless failed efforts before this one, my nipples were raw and bleeding already. Not to mention what was happening to them now that this hungry little boy was drinking like his life depended on it.

This woman said what a wonderful thing it was that he was drinking. I agreed, it was indeed wonderful, but not exactly something that I could do in Saudi

Arabia. I wasn't able to sit at the airport or in a shopping mall and strip down just so my baby could feed.

Her parting words were, "I'll pray for you." My son, from then on, drank from a bottle. Easiest choice I'd made.

As soon as I'd decided to bottle feed, he started packing on the weight and he was as good as gold. Every four hours on the dot, wake up, change, feed, and sleep again. He was amazing on the flight home to Saudi. We'd had to apply for a rapid passport and visa stamps. Which meant a day trip in London. So much fun. Mum had come with me, we had passport photos done, he looked like a little Yoda with a scrunched up face. We got him on the train and made our way up to the city, Mum had already decided we were going to get a taxi to the passport office, but as I was still a relatively new mum, I hadn't mastered the pushchair yet. Lots of fumbling, taxi drivers giggling and a few choice words from me and we managed our goal and had a stamped, certified visa and passport. Nothing appeared to be all that easy, but I always managed to make the choice to see the funny side of everything.

The next couple of years were pretty straight forward. I had everything I had ever wanted. An amazing husband who seemed to love me just as I was, warts and all. And a son, that couldn't have been easier. He could be a bit of a nightmare when it came to putting him to bed, I couldn't leave the room until he was actually asleep. It took me a minute to work out how to handle it. I would sit on the floor, next to his cot, with my hand on his bum and wiggle gently. He'd eventually fall asleep and I would get up to leave. This is where I perfected my ninja skills. I became stealth like to a level I didn't think existed. A lot of the time, he'd bloody wake up though, so it took a lot of patience and skill. We did eventually get him out of this habit when we bought him a "big boy bed".

CHAPTER FIFTEEN

"YOU DID NOT WAKE UP TODAY TO BE MEDIOCRE."
—UNKNOWN.

Not long after I had my son, I realised there was a problem with my lady bits. I knew after my delivery that I was going to be sore, but this continued and amplified any time I came into contact with skin. It got to the point where it would go away completely, then skin would come into contact with me and my lady garden suddenly became so sore it felt like I'd had a fight with a cactus. For a week or so after contact, I hurt so badly that showering or going to the toilet was a real challenge. I would cry every single time and had to really psyche myself up. It became almost unbearable.

I was referred to a doctor, a specialist doctor, a gynaecologist, and finally a skin specialist. I came across a gynaecologist who was at the top of his field. A super specialist, whatever that is. I'd met with him, told him my symptoms and then we discussed treatments and options. I went for surgery with him to be tested for cancer of the vulva.

I remember vividly the day I got the call that I didn't have cancer. Mum and I had taken my son on a walk through a forest, one we've done often, and whilst in the thick of a muddy path, my phone rang. The doctor simply said, "It's not cancer." I don't remember the rest of the call, but I do remember screaming at the top of my lungs that I was clear. I went for a follow up appointment and the doctor told me that although I was cancer free, I did have an allergy to aloe vera. So maybe I was getting all the flare ups because I was using products with aloe in them. I cut out everything that had this nasty little plant in. It's amazing how many things use aloe vera.

There was still a problem though. This pain that happened when I had "contact" with anything. Add in to that, sex was excruciating. My doctor had told me that it was psychosomatic. The contact pain and any other pain was all in my head. Great, it can join the rest of the crap I had in my head. I did what I did best. I just got on with it and accepted it as my new reality.

Fast forward a year or so and I'd fallen pregnant again. I had two psychogenic non-epileptic seizures at seventeen weeks. I was run down and tired and I'd just got over a nasty cold, I'd also flown back to Saudi following a visit to Mum and Dad's, with a toddler.

I was fine, just tired. The rest of my pregnancy with what turned out to be my daughter, was non-eventful. My husband and I had decided to have her in Saudi. My care had been so awful in the UK that it was a nerve-wracking choice, but an easy one. We were able to pick the hospital and then the doctor who would see me all the way up to delivery.

I was induced on the 10th June 2009. I had a beautiful suite, because God help anyone if I was seen by someone other than a doctor or my husband. A doctor came into my room, at the insistence of Robert, and did a little poke around to see if the induction had worked at all, turns out, she broke my waters "Quite by mistake, Madam." And break my waters she did. It was kind of like the Hoover Dam bursting. I have never known anything like it, it just kept coming. A choice was made to get me into delivery. But it wasn't as straight forward as one might think.

Robert had to rush down to the insurance office to get the paperwork sorted out for the epidural, while I was simultaneously rushed through a couple of sets of doors, through a badly lit corridor, all with my abaya over my head and body so nobody would see me, easy enough to cover me while I'm in a wheelchair, and deposited into a single room, albeit unceremoniously. I waited for Robert and as soon as he entered the room, I had an incredible urge to push. He started panicking saying it was too soon. That I can't push. You try telling a heavily pregnant woman, in active labour, that she can't push. Yeah, fuck no.

He ran out of the room and just to get him back into the room, so that he wouldn't see any other patients, the doctors and nurses came rushing in. Sure enough, the doctor took one look at my lady garden and suddenly, the end of the bed vanished, stirrups went in, and I was dragged like a piece of meat towards the end of the bed. Feet were shoved into the metal devices now standing pride of place down at the business end.

The doctor who had come to do my epidural, sat me up as best as he could so he could administer the test medicine. At the same time, contraction number two arrived like a long lost cousin who wanted nothing more than to be the centre of attention. He got the medicine in and the third contraction hit.

Our daughter was born on that third contraction, she appeared out of my cooter like a champagne cork leaves a bottle. Our son had thoughtfully already paved the way for her.

They pretty much forced me to breastfeed while I was in the hospital, I had already decided that I didn't want to do that. I'd learned with my son, that being able to see what our babies are drinking and how much, can be really beneficial. We persevered and Robert snuck bottles of formula into the hospital.

The day after she was born, a little over twelve hours old, two nurses came into my room and said "We take her now." I was confused, she'd already had the necessary vaccinations for that country, so what could they be taking her for? The answer was not what I was expecting. "We take her get ears pierced and you know…" No, I didn't know. Between Robert and I, and the nurses, we managed to work out that they wanted to take my beautiful baby girl to be circumcised. "Er, fuck no, you don't." Very simple, very pointed response from me. They had no idea what to do. No one had said no to them before, not for this.

They left the room looking like they were about to lose their jobs. At that point, I honestly didn't care. No way were they going to touch my baby. I didn't let her out of my sight after that. Not until we left the hospital, and even then I was super nervous about not being able to actually see her.

CHAPTER SIXTEEN

"YOUR TIME IS LIMITED, SO DON'T WASTE IT LIVING SOMEONE ELSE'S LIFE." — STEVE JOBS.

I remember the first time my son told me that he loved me. I had bought our daughter home a couple of days before, my mum was still staying with us to help out a little. She'd got him ready for his morning at nursery and as he was leaving the house, holding tightly to Granny's hand, he turned around, looked me dead in the eye and said, "I love you, Mummy."

That right there. Remember when I said earlier about having a purpose? This was mine. Being a mother and a wife. My purpose. I suddenly felt complete and worthwhile.

I was happy. Truly, genuinely happy and I let every single person I came across know it. I was living my life the way I wanted to live it, without abandon.

Chapter Seventeen

"If you don't like the path you're walking, start paving another one." — Dolly Parton.

The quote above was wrong, it wasn't that easy. For so long, I'd tried paving other paths, I'd hated the path I was on so long ago. Now I was finally on a path I loved being on. I was happy, but someone, somewhere decided I needed to be on a different path.

We left Saudi and moved to Dubai. Not going to lie, I wasn't a fan. Too many tourists and too much commercialisation. I lived with it though and made the best I could of the situation I found myself in. We lived an extraordinary life there and made some friends, none of whom I'm in touch with since we left. Being an Expat, you become very transient, you make friends easily, but rarely form attachments because you know that ultimately, you're going to leave. It hurts less this way.

I'm going to skip forward a couple of years, because frankly, there is only so much a person can read about the affluent lifestyle a person has when they're living in a place like Dubai.

We moved to Kuwait in 2011. We lived in a massive house which had been split into three separate homes. We had the second floor. I hated this place even more than Dubai.

Kuwait was the love child if Saudi and Dubai had a baby. Endless sandstorms while shopping for Louis Vuitton and buying alcohol in a blacked out shop and leaving with your naughty purchase in a brown paper bag.

I remember my son coming running through the apartment to me one day telling me that his sister was blue. Mothering instincts kicked in and I immediately start thinking about my emergency plan to get her to the closest hospital. Wait, where was the fucking hospital?

I followed him to the kitchen so he could show me his blue sister. What you need to remember, in countries in the Middle East, the floors, ceiling and walls are typically white because of the heat.

The walls, floor, and ceiling in my kitchen, all surrounding my kitchen table, were now not white. Yep, they were blue. As was my daughter. From head to toe, blue. She'd stripped out of her clothes, with the help of her accommodating big brother, and stood, proud as punch in her nappy, blue. No matter how much I bathed her, scrubbed her, she stayed various shades of blue for about a week and a half. The reason she was blue in the first place? The kids had been given the task of painting me a picture, and had free access to our supply of paints, while I went to do a quick chore. Entirely my fault.

Regardless, life was good. Settled, happy.

CHAPTER EIGHTEEN

IF YOU ARE STRUGGLING TODAY, REMEMBER THIS:
"YOU HAVE SURVIVED EVERYTHING YOU'VE GONE
THROUGH UP TO THIS POINT. THE BEST DAY OF
YOUR LIFE IS STILL YET TO COME. THERE ARE
STILL PEOPLE YOU HAVEN'T MET, AND THINGS YOU
HAVEN'T EXPERIENCED. YOU CAN DO THIS." —
UNKNOWN.

Just when you think you've got your shit together, that life is finally content, happy, the Universe throws you a curveball.

The problems with my lady garden were still very much there. They were getting worse day-by-day, and there didn't seem to be a damn thing I could do about it. I think I'd just resigned myself to the fact that this was how it was meant to be for me. It wasn't something you discussed with friends and family, and honestly, it wasn't something that I wanted to go and see anyone about, especially in any of the Middle Eastern countries we'd lived in.

I realised that I'd made a choice. A choice to just live with it and adapt. It's what I did. On reflection, choices were a huge part of my life. I'd grown up being given the "choices lecture" by my dad, so they were something I was familiar with.

Some of the choices I'd made weren't great, and they'd honestly, led me down dark paths. But after I'd married Robert, had the kids, I'd decided that I was not going to let life get me down. I made that choice. No matter what life throws at me, I was going to choose to be better. Do better.

I had no idea how much I was going to have to rely on that mindset.

We flew back to the UK, permanently, in December 2011. Robert had lost his job, so we packed up our house, and had it shipped back to England. As we didn't have anywhere to live at the time we moved, I had to find somewhere fast. Thankfully, house rentals were easy to find back then, so I signed all the paperwork and sent the relevant details to the shipping company. We weren't going to get the shipment until at least February, so we were staying with Mum and Dad until we took over the new place.

My lower body pain had become a normal part of my life, and I'd almost resigned myself to the fact that this was just how it was going to be for the rest of my life. Until one day, my mum asked me why I was walking like that and why did it look like I'd been crying. It was almost as if she'd turned a dial or something and opened the flood gates. Out it all came. The pain I'd been suffering with, the after effects of anything even remotely "naughty". My mum isn't typically the type of person to makes waves. She did that day. I made an appointment to see our family doctor, who took one look at me and referred me back to the specialist I'd seen so many years before.

I had my appointment with the specialist and, after describing my symptoms to him, without any further investigations, he told me I had endometriosis. I asked him what could be done about it and how could I stop it coming back? He explained that he could laser off the endo, from my tubes, and to stop it coming back, he could sterilise me. (Twelve years on and this still stings a little.) I told him that, okay, while I was going to go ahead with this, I was being sterilised because I *needed* to be, and not because I *wanted* to be, and to make it absolutely clear with him and in my notes. He said he understood and I watched as he furiously wrote in my file.

I went into hospital in July 2012 to have the procedure. When I woke up, the doctor who'd done the operation, not the one who I'd had the appointment with, came in to see me. I asked how it all went. She'd told me that my fallopian tubes were beautiful and healthy and there had been no evidence of any disease. I remember telling her how wonderful and what a relief because I hadn't needed to be sterilised. "Oh no, we did that anyway. It was what you wanted." I wasn't very nice or polite when I asked her to leave.

It won't shock anyone at this point to learn that the pain of contact and sex, was absolutely still there, and frankly getting worse each and every time.

Three days before my birthday in 2012, I went back to the specialist for my post-op appointment. I'm not going to lie; I did go into the appointment with a little attitude. I was angry. Really angry. I'd desperately wanted to be a surrogate for my friend, I'd loved being pregnant but knew I didn't want another baby of my own. Why not pass that gift onto someone else?

He explained to me that even though my tubes had been clear of endo, that clearly meant, because I was still having so many problems, that it was in my womb. Still no investigative procedures. So what now?

Apparently I had two options. I could have hormone stoppers for three months to see if that worked, it would force me into early menopause, or, I could have a partial hysterectomy. Take everything except my ovaries, basically.

I told him that he'd already screwed me over as a female sterilisation couldn't be reversed, we may as well go for the latter option of the hysterectomy. I did not want to go through menopause at thirty-six.

In January 2013, I went into hospital to have the procedure done. All I had to show for having the essence of being a woman removed, was a slightly beaten-up lady garden. They'd taken it all out through the South exit. A little like a vacuum. They had made two tiny incisions in my belly so they could insert cameras to see what they were doing.

It took a little getting used to. I no longer felt like a woman, but I obviously wasn't a man. What the hell was I? Don't get me wrong, I'm not an idiot. I knew I was still female, but I definitely no longer felt like a woman.

A few days after I'd been released from hospital, I found myself back there for an emergency appointment. I'd developed a massive blood clot and bruising around on of the incisions in my belly button. The doctor took one look at it, and simply said, "So you have." She rubbed something on my belly, I still don't know what, smiled at me and left. That was it.

I had my post-op in the April, a few months later. Low and behold the pain was all still very much there. By this point, having actually decided to seek medical help, I was desperate. I didn't want to live like this anymore.

I didn't see my normal doctor at this follow up. It was one of the registrars. I was excited to find out the results of the surgery. He explained to me that my womb was perfectly healthy, and there were no signs of any endo at all, in anything they'd taken out. Nothing. No endo, no cancer, no disease of any kind.

I have no shame in admitting that at that exact moment, I dropped to my knees, in the doctor's office, and cried. I cried and begged him to help me. What was wrong with me? Why can't I be intimate with my husband without being in imaginable pain?

His answer shocked me to my core. "I'm sorry, there is nothing more we can do to help you." And then he walked out.

Chapter Nineteen

"Give a girl the right shoes, and she can conquer the world." — Marilyn Monroe.

Robert held me together at this point. Between him and my mum, they kept me ticking over. Long enough that I could get my own shit together and walk in a straight line. I'd moved in with Mum and Dad again with the kids, as Robert had gone back to Iraq where he was working at the time. He was doing shifts of three months on, one month off. It was hard, but we managed. As always. I knew I had to get into a new mindset. I made the choice then and there, I was going to accept that now I was a glorified blow-up doll and that I had two ping pong balls in a pillowcase (my ovaries).

It was on one of his rotations where he was away, that I made probably one of the worst choices I've ever made. I think back on it now and know exactly why I did it. An ex of mine had reached out to me saying hi, we started chatting and then all of a sudden, the conversation became sexually explicit. Not my finest hour, but at the time, I wanted, desperately, to feel enough. To feel wanted, attractive. Ever since the surgery, I had felt... empty. Not quite a woman, not quite whole. Robert had been amazing and everything I could have ever asked for, but to hear that you're attractive from someone, who I believed didn't have an obligation to say it, was at the time, so much more.

Robert panicked and came home almost immediately. Did we need to talk? Work on our marriage? No.

There was nothing wrong with our marriage. But there was something wrong with me. The impact of the hysterectomy had damaged me, almost beyond repair, but psychologically not physically. I mean, the physical damage was still evident, but the mental damage, still affects me to this day, to a point.

We talked, a lot. About everything, anything, and nothing. I explained why I'd done what I'd done, why I felt the need to get some sort of validation from someone else, that my husband was absolutely enough, just at that time, I needed something else.

We moved on, stronger than ever.

Chapter Twenty

"THINK LIKE A QUEEN. A QUEEN IS NOT AFRAID TO FAIL. FAILURE IS ANOTHER STEPPINGSTONE TO GREATNESS." — OPRAH WINFREY.

I had gone into the local town to get some supplies that we wanted to take with us when we moved over to America. I was walking down one of the side streets. The sky was grey, and it was trying desperately to rain. You could feel the occasional splatter of a wayward rain drop land somewhere on your body.

Once I'd stopped looking at the sky, remembering that day in 1993, so long ago, but something I always remembered when the sky looked the way it did, I looked back towards street level to be greeted by one of the things that stopped me going into that town. One of the boys who'd violated me in the worst way was standing directly in front of me.

I'd seen him around town over the years, but I'd always managed to avoid him, crossing the street, diving into the closest shop, ducking behind a car. Anything that would mean I could avoid eye contact, let along conversation. The last time I'd spoken to him, was when he'd bragged to his friends in a pub, quite loudly, how I was the slag who'd had attempted rape put on his criminal record. It had been marked down as "attempted" because of his age. Apparently a thirteen-year-old wasn't capable of something as heinous as rape.

It'd taken me a split second, a split second to make a choice. I was working in the pub at the time and had an armful of pint glasses. I took off the top one, and in the flick of a wrist, I smashed it across the top of his head. Not my proudest moment, but right then, it felt good. Not because I'd caused him harm, but because I'd made him look stupid in front of his whole group of friends.

Back to having him right in front of me in the street. Right then I suddenly decided that I was not going to be a victim anymore. I was no longer going to allow him, and the choices that he made, determine how I was going to live my life. I had given too much of myself to him already.

I looked him dead in the eye, straightened my shoulders and said very simply, but with more confidence than I thought possible, "I forgive you." I turned on my heel and walked away with my head held higher than I ever had before.

I had acceptance, but more importantly, I had forgiveness. I couldn't have cared less if he accepted my apology. It wasn't for him. It was for me.

CHAPTER TWENTY-ONE

"BE THE CHANGE THAT YOU WISH TO SEE IN THE WORLD." — MAHATMA GANDHI.

In 2015, we moved to America. I wasn't as nervous moving here as I was when we moved to the Middle East. I very soon found out why. It was home. I've always said that every single person on the planet "fits" somewhere. We've been really lucky, and because of Robert's job, we've travelled. I knew, when we arrived in America, we were home.

It took some adjusting, we'd moved to Colorado, Mile High City. They weren't kidding. I was not ready for the extreme altitude change.

Robert had gone over ahead of me and the kids. They wanted to stay at school for as long as they could, and I needed to pack up the house, sort out visas, all the boring mundane stuff. He went looking for houses and we'd FaceTime whenever he thought he'd found a good one. We did, eventually. A beautiful detached, four-bedroom home, that was frankly bigger than anything I'd ever lived in before.

The kids and I flew out on October 28th, 2015. We were staying in temporary accommodation until we could get the keys for the new rental the following Sunday.

It was on this particular Sunday, that I realised just how bad the altitude problem was. We had been furniture shopping a couple of days before and it was due to be delivered on the Sunday morning. But we overslept. So we get a phone call that the delivery guys were at the house, but where were we? Shit, shit, shit.

We gave them the code for the garage, and they dumped everything in there. Two double beds, one was one of those high sleeper things, and a Californian King-sized bed, all with mattresses. There were some other bits as well, but they became irrelevant. The delivery guys were supposed to build our new beds so that we were able to sleep the first night in our new house that night.

I'm a bit of a DIY enthusiast. Always have been and I decided that it wasn't going to be a problem if the delivery guys just left our stuff. I'd put it together. Robert and I started taking each piece of furniture into the house. By the time I got halfway up the stairs, I thought I'd run a marathon. I could not work out why I was so out of breath, and apparently unfit. By the time we got our bed up the stairs, I thought my lungs were going to jump out of my chest and tell me to fuck off. We did eventually get it all done and spent our first night of many in our new house.

The kids started school, my husband was happy, and life was good. I'm not actually all that good with change, so when any big change happens, my recurring nightmares come back with a vengeance. They can be pretty violent and always along the same theme. The rape when I was sixteen, the bullying, the psychological abuse, all of it. On a never-ending stream set to repeat.

It was exhausting. But the more I settled into my new world, the less the nightmares came.

We did become settled. One day just rolled into another, and like I said before, we had found our home. The place in the world where we fit.

The kids had adapted really well in school, but it was clear my son was struggling with some aspects. At the suggestion of his school, I had him tested for ADHD. A diagnosis came back crystal clear and we now had a reason why he was always on the go and unable to focus sometimes. We started on a medication, and it took us three or four until we found one that suited him.

Chapter Twenty-Two

"Follow your dreams, believe in yourself, never give up." —Damien Thomas.

We found ourselves moving again in 2017. Robert had been offered a type of promotion within the same company, and now we were moving to Washington.

We'd bought a 1984 Campervan. Robert thought it was the best thing since sliced bread. I thought it was a relic. But it served a purpose, and I convinced myself that maybe it would make the road trip a little more adventurous for us all.

We packed up the house, sent that off on its way and then set off ourselves. We saw some of the most breath-taking scenery that I've ever seen. Nothing like we had in the UK, land that went for miles, much further than the eye could see. Farmhouses dotted throughout the land and fields. I found myself wishing that I could one day live a life like that. A beautiful farmhouse with a country style kitchen, and chickens. Why did I suddenly want chickens so badly?

It took us three days to find our way to Washington. A couple of minor repairs along the way. We'd arrived at the edge of Idaho, parked up for the night and a break in driving at a service station. Once the kids were both settled, I'd taken the dog out for a tiddle before bed. I went back in and told Robert that I could smell petrol. He instantly came out and said that it was probably just the RV cooling down and that it was a little old. He knew what he was talking about, so I didn't question it again.

We woke up the following morning, and again took the dog out. There was the RV sitting in a pool of petrol. There was a massive puddle under the wheels and when I shouted for Robert, he came out and did a little investigating. Turns out, one of the fuel lines had split. He patched it up and we made our way to our friends' house in Idaho, so that he could fix it properly.

I'm not sure how, but we eventually made it to Washington and the RV park we'd reserved before we were able to pick up the keys for our new house.

Washington was stunning. Green everywhere, beautiful winding roads and friendly faces everywhere I turned. It reinforced everything I'd felt living in Colorado. I was home. This country was beyond amazing, and I adored living here.

Chapter Twenty-Three

"Sometimes life is about risking everything for a dream no one can see but you." — Unknown.

When the shit hits the fan, sometimes you see it coming, but more often, you get blindsided by a storm so large, you don't know how to get through the turmoil.

My kids both started at the local elementary school. We'd found an amazing house in a tiny little backwater town. They were happy. I was happy, my marriage was solid. Everything was perfect. Until it wasn't.

We'd arrived in Washington in the August 2017. My daughter was eight and my son was ten. In the December that same year, my daughter went through Precocious Puberty. Basically, she started her period. Full blown. Excruciating pain, mood swings, heavy monthly bleeding. My heart broke for her, but outwardly I remained strong because that's what she needed me to be.

I went out and bought all the things I thought she might need, pads, heating pads, painkillers, and of course, plenty of ice cream. Periods are hard at the best of times, but when you're eight? That sucked huge, hairy donkey balls for her.

It became our normal. Every month, like clockwork, we'd deal with the shit show that arrived. She was amazing, missed some school, but nothing we couldn't deal with.

Chapter Twenty-Four

"No matter what's happening, choose to be happy. Don't focus on what's wrong. Find something positive in your life." —Joel Osteen.

Here comes the start of the storm. Do you see it? No? Neither did I. I hit me so hard, that I struggled to comprehend, and I had no idea how to help my beautiful girl.

Between March 2018 and June 2018, my daughter's breasts grew from what you'd expect an eight-year-old to have, to a fairly massive 34i. In two months. We took her to see a specialist, three actually, who all said the same thing. She's a super-fast grower. It's just one of those things. Kids all grow at different rates.

We did have a bone growth scan done on her. She was showing to have the bone growth of a twelve-year-old, at eight. Four years above her age. I asked if that was a cause of concern and all the doctors we came across, assured me that it was nothing to worry about.

I trusted what I was hearing. American doctors, so I believed, were some of the best in the world. Right?

But a person can get through most physical problems. It takes courage and strength, but it can be done. We went out and bought her bras, ones that would actually fit her properly, and changed her wardrobe slightly. Just with clothes that she would feel more comfortable in.

But what no one warns you about, is the mental trauma something like this puts on a person. You don't get warned about the choices other kids make at the expense of your beautiful child.

When we'd got back to the UK, we eventually found out that she has a very rare medical condition called Gigantomastia. There's a deformity in her breast tissue. After a year of fighting with various medical professionals and making countless phone calls, she had a breast reduction with one of the best paediatric cosmetic surgeons in the world. On the day of surgery, she measured at a 38JJ. They took 7lbs off each side and took her down to a 38C. When she woke up from her operation and saw them for the first time, her first words were, "They're perfect." And they were. That operation was in July 2021, we're now in 2023 and they've grown a decent amount again. We have another appointment in the next couple of months.

Chapter Twenty-Five

"Life moves on... Whether you choose to move on and take a chance in the unknown, or stay behind, locked in the past, thinking of what could've been." — My Dear Valentine.

I'm not going to go into the rest of her story. It's not my story to tell. I have her permission to say what I want, but this book is about helping people, whoever you are reading this, helping you to understand that choice, no matter how hard, is always offering one a better way out and a better way to deal with one's demons. It sounds easy. It isn't. It's actually one of the hardest things I've ever had to do.

It does get easier. It really does. I know that sometimes, you'll get thrown a trauma, a life challenge, whatever, it'll feel like the world is coming to an end, you don't know how to deal with it. How much more can you take?

But in those moments, take a breath. Make a choice to take a breath. Make a choice to take a step forward. Just one. It's enough for now. But those breaths and those steps become more and more each time.

We'd moved back to the UK in December 2019. Living in America, we knew about the "At Will" bullshit. A company can let you go with no rhyme or reason.

My husband was expensive for them, and with cutbacks imminent, he was one of the obvious choices. They had messed up our Green Card paperwork and as a result, we had no choice but to pack up our house and leave. Leave the one place I'd felt at home. The one place I'd ever been where I genuinely felt like I fitted in.

We decided to move back to a specific area to be closer to my parents. I'd always lived in this area, so it was familiar to me and felt safe. Or so I thought.

I'd been away for nearly five years, people had moved on and essentially, I was no longer a part of anything here. I'd had an idea in my mind what it was going to look like when I got back, I was adamant that the friends I'd made via the children before we had left, were still going to be my friends and that they were going to welcome me with open arms. I was wrong, there was no warm welcome, and there were no friends.

I reached out to a decent sized group of people to reconnect. Some were willing, some weren't. The ones who were willing to meet up again, suddenly drifted away.

In comes the paranoia. The feelings of self-doubt, am I good enough? What's wrong with me? Why do I not have any friends that actually want to hang out? The feelings that I thought I'd squashed so long ago, put to the back of my mind, resurfaced with a vengeance.

I missed America terribly. I missed my friends there; those people just accepted me absolutely as I was. Flaws and all. They understood that I came with a little baggage and accepted me regardless. No questions. They supported me anyway and my God, did we laugh.

CHAPTER TWENTY-SIX

"AN ONION HAS MANY LAYERS, BUT THE BEST IS ON THE INSIDE, JUST LIKE YOU." —ACWM.

In America in 2019, I was diagnosed with Stage 2 Melanoma. Skin cancer. Not something I'd ever thought I'd have to say. My friends rallied around me. Offering support and crying with me when I needed to. They helped my husband when I'd had to go in for surgery and then helped us all when I was recovering and letting my new reality sink in.

I was seriously incredibly lucky. We'd caught it really early, so surgery cut out a decent chunk of my arm and cleared all the margins and took lymph nodes to make sure the disease hadn't spread. I didn't have to have chemo or radiotherapy. I thank God every single day for that. All I have to do now is have regular mole mapping appointments to make sure there isn't anything sinister going on. Next year, I will officially be in remission.

Going through the cancer, no matter what level or stage, is brutal. Never mind the physical aspect of it, what it does mentally is just as hard. You suddenly find yourself questioning everything. Everything. Your purpose, your life, your choices, your mortality. One assumes that we'll live until a ripe old age and that it won't be cut short. Suddenly you get blindsided with something you never saw coming, and it makes you realise that there are certain things that are not in your control.

What cancer did do for me, is compound my thoughts that I know my worth, I know where I belong and what my priorities are.

My children and my husband are everything to me. That hasn't changed, and anyone who sees me on any kind of social media would know that my family are my world.

Cancer changed my perception of friends. I no longer tolerate bullshit. I will gladly accept you and all that you have to offer, without judgement. But, and yes there's a but, if you cross me, upset anyone in my family significantly enough, I will walk away without a second thought. I know who I am, and I know what I stand for and believe in enough.

Chapter Twenty-Seven

"When you saw only one set of footprints, it was then that I carried you." — Footprints in the Sand, Ryan Hart.

My Faith has always been a huge part of my life. I've struggled with it once or twice, but it remained strong. I've always believed that there was a higher power of sorts. For me, that was God. I wasn't some born-again Christian. I didn't attend church regularly, but I felt that I didn't need to actually go to church to worship what I believed in.

My Faith is what has got me through some of the hardest times in my life. That was until a day in June 2022, when I was up at the hospital again. My daughter was struggling with hallucinations and serious suicidal ideations. She was already actively self-harming, and the threat to "unalive" herself was very real. This particular visit was number twelve that year.

I had a routine that I followed whenever we found ourselves at our local hospital. I'd get her settled into the children's ward, make sure she was asleep, and then make my way down to the Chapel to pray. It was something that I loved doing. It was a place where I felt peace amongst the chaos that was happening. Somewhere I felt like I belonged when I felt helpless and unable to cope with what was happening to my daughter.

Whenever I walked into the Chapel, I was surrounded by a hug, a warm and accepting feeling that made me feel like I could cope with anything that was thrown my way. When I left, I had confidence that I could help my baby and knew I'd be able to get her through whatever trauma she was dealing with.

On this particular visit, her thoughts, her demons, were the worst they'd ever been. We'd hit what I now know, was the peak of her troubles. I went through the same routines as before. Get her assessed, to the ward, asleep, and then I'd make my way down to the Chapel.

But when I reached that sacred door, I wasn't filled with love and hope. I was suddenly filled with an overwhelming feeling of rage, and despair. I remember brushing it off and thinking that it would be fine once I actually walked in and sat down.

It wasn't fine. The feelings of rage and despair strengthened, and hate decided to join this particular party. It really frightened me because I'd never before felt these negative emotions so strongly in this sacred place. I felt completely consumed by them, I wanted to hurt someone or something. I simply couldn't understand why, if God was real, why He would cause so much pain and hurt onto my beautiful daughter.

I started crying, gut wrenching sobs that nearly broke me. I don't remember getting back up to the ward, I do remember feeling the strongest urge to leave the Chapel and get back up to her. It was a very sudden, very desperate need. I had to be with her. When I got back up to the ward a nurse took one look at me and started to move. A flurry of activity happened, and I was given a seat and a glass of water. I was having a panic attack. I knew this but I couldn't make my words work.

The nurses were amazing, they knew me pretty well by that point and knew that this wasn't normal behaviour for me. They told me that my daughter had been fine, hadn't woken up and was sleeping peacefully. They got me to calm down and I tried desperately to explain to them that I'd suddenly lost my Faith and I was scared.

I still don't have it back fully. There is something there, but not how it used to be for me. I'm okay with that. Of course, I'd love to have it back how it was before all this, but I'll settle for what I have now and trust that in time, I'll get it back.

Chapter Twenty-Eight

"I BELIEVE IN MYSELF... SO ANYTHING IS POSSIBLE." —UNKNOWN.

Being the way that I am can be incredibly lonely. But the Universe has a funny way of showing a person their worth. I would meet people and form bonds with them that are still growing strong to this day. I currently have a couple that are unbreakable at the moment. There's always the worry in the back of my mind that one day, even those will eventually fade away. But for the moment, I'm loving these friendships for what they are.

There comes a point in life, I think, where you have to decide if you're going to succumb and forever be a victim of your past or stand up to your truth. To be the person you truly are.

I've always believed that people who abuse, in any way, people who assault, again in any way, people who bully, or generally anyone who has a negative impact on your life, those people make their own choices.

People have made a choice to do harm to me. That's absolutely on them and no longer my burden to bear. It never was. But growing up, I strongly believed that if someone did me harm, it was my problem to fix. It never was.

Once I'd realised that, my world suddenly got smaller, and safer. My world became just that, my world. I decided to let in who I wanted and said goodbye to who I wanted.

CHAPTER TWENTY-NINE

"YOU AREN'T STRUGGLING WITH DEPRESSION; DEPRESSION IS STRUGGLING WITH YOU." — ACWM.

D epression has tried to kick my arse throughout most of my life. Mental health is never something to scoff at. It's an illness that you can't see, you can't touch.

Some of the choices, actually a lot, I've made have made my mental health worse in a lot of ways. I own that. Completely, but I've also decided to take back control of my life. Make better choices. Live and love completely.

Choices. No matter how hard they seem, no matter how impossible that choice may seem, take a minute, and breathe. Make the choice for you, the one that best fits your life in that moment.

It's really important for anyone reading this book to remember that this is your life that you're living and the choices that you make, will impact you completely. The choices of other people may have impacts on you, but then you get to choose how to take that moving forward. If you need to turn it around, do it. If you need to walk away from whatever situation, do it.

It is your choice to live your life how you want to live it. Take the steps to make your life the best version that it can be.

You deserve to be happy; I deserve to be happy.

CHAPTER THIRTY

"DON'T FOLLOW YOUR DREAMS, CHASE THEM." — UNKNOWN.

Finally, I have found "my people". I was at my lowest last year, after I'd lost my Faith, my daughter was struggling, my son was struggling with his diagnosis of ASD. I decided that I could no longer cope with the turmoil going on both inside and outside of my head.

Life was proving to be getting harder day by day and I just didn't know who to turn to anymore. I was desperately trying to find a way out. A way to cope, and I couldn't come up with one.

I made a date; I made a plan. So now I knew when, where and how I was going to "leave". I'm not going into detail about this time, because I simply don't need to.

What I can tell you though, is that the love of my husband, the love of my children, and a really random video saved my life. Literally.

Let me tell you about that random video because it's changed the course of my life. It's given me purpose, and if you're reading this book and have got this far, chances are, that you too have been through some sort of trauma.

I saw a video of a boy who had been sexually assaulted by a member of his family. In the description that came with the video it detailed a group that he'd started on Facebook for survivors of sexual assault. I reached out to him in the hope that I could find help and support for my daughter. Not for me, for her. It was literally my last ditched attempt to be useful and find some help for her.

I wasn't expecting him to reply because he'd had an enormous number of comments on his video and I didn't think he actually read his messages. But I was ever hopeful.

Two weeks after I'd sent the message, ten days before *my* date, I received a reply from him. We started talking about my daughter and his group and he invited me to join. So I accepted and started reading the group posts and their comments.

You know that feeling you get when you're suddenly hit by a realisation? Yeah, I felt that so suddenly, so strongly that I cried. I cried for my daughter, I cried for me. I just sat and sobbed. It was in those conversations that I realised that I would never leave my family, my husband, my children, and it was in those conversations with this group and this guy, that I found my worth and my place. I'd found people just like me. None of us have been through the exact same things, but we've all been through something similar. Where someone else has made a choice that has had a direct impact on us.

I had something that I'd so desperately wanted for so long. Support. Unwavering support.

CHAPTER THIRTY-ONE

"PEOPLE CRY NOT BECAUSE THEY'RE WEAK, BUT BECAUSE THEY'VE BEEN STRONG FOR TOO LONG." — JOHNNY DEPP.

I don't want a single person to read this and think I've had the worst life. I haven't. Yes, I've been through my fair share of shit. But it's mine, and I know that there are people out there who have had to deal with far worse than I have. But it's important for everyone to know that no matter what trauma you go through, life is worth living. Regardless.

Reach out to someone, talk to someone. If someone tells you they are there for you, believe them. Lean on them. Seek professional help, go to support groups, and surround yourself with people who have been through a trauma, seek solace and guidance from them.

You are not alone. Please don't suffer in silence. You are not a burden, and you have a story to share.

Be real and be yourself. You are worthy of love. But most importantly, do not be silenced. Giving a voice to trauma, to pain, means you take back your power. Be Powerful.

CHAPTER THIRTY-TWO

My family are very aware that I'm writing this book. There have been a lot of feelings and emotions that have come up whilst I've been going through the process.

I've written a little about my kids, but I haven't gone into significant detail about what they've been through. It simply isn't my story to tell.

However, my beautiful, strong daughter, who we christened Abie, wanted to write something of her own, and I'm beyond privileged that she wanted to add it in here.

She's not had an easy childhood. Because of the choices of others, certain things have happened to her that have had a massive effect on her life.

She has gone through all sorts of different ideas on how she wants to be within her life. She doesn't feel that she's had a childhood, or not much of one anyway. So, I'm happy to support whatever she wants to feel at any given time.

With her mental health, I've found it a real struggle to help her deal with it. I help where I can and give advice, I hold her sometimes when she cries. But more importantly, I've talked her through how I've coped with invasive and intrusive thoughts.

Choice. I learned a few years ago that with choice, you can turn your life around. You can make the choice and change everything. It's not easy to do it, it's not easy to learn how to do it, but with perseverance and a little patience, she's getting there.

She once said that she wants to be like me, to learn how to put the past behind her like I have. It both terrifies me and makes me proud in equal measure. I wished for so long that I'd had someone there for me, who could give me these lessons growing up, so that I might not have made some of the choices that I've made. But I didn't and I learned for myself.

I still have days when I struggle, where my feelings just get the better of me. But I choose to let myself have those days. It's okay to not be happy and positive every single day. But make the choice to understand that you can have a bad day, but tomorrow, you're going to straighten your crown and move forward. One step and one breath at a time.

Finding out what Abie has gone through in her short life, nearly destroyed me initially. I internalised it and made her problems, my problems. I took her pain as my own. It took someone completely random to make me see that her mental health had nothing to do with me. It was hers and hers alone.

It was then that I decided to help her the best way I could while she navigated her thoughts and urges.

I'd patch her up when she cut and held her when she cried. Sometimes I cried with her, and then we brushed ourselves off and continued with our lives.

It was only when it dawned on me the things that she did, were out of my control. If she was going to self-harm or try and end her life, if she really wanted to do it, there wasn't going to be a damn thing I could do about it. I talk with her all the time about choices and that her life won't always be this hard, she will always have days where she struggles, but the good days will out-weigh the bad.

I have told my son the same thing. He is now sixteen and has a diagnosis of ADHD and Autism. He's high functioning, and so clever he nearly outsmarts Robert and his grandfather.

He struggles daily with impulsivity, thoughts that run rampant in his brain, "Should I put this metal bowl in the microwave?" and before he has even processed the thought, he finds the bowl already in the microwave. He has struggled terribly with his sister's mental health. Not being able to help her like he wants to, she pushes him away more often than not and that de-values him and his feelings. Watching him navigating that, hurts my soul. He's very private and keeps his feelings to himself a lot of the time. He knows that I struggle with my own mental health, and as a result he doesn't want to burden me with thoughts and feelings that he has. No matter how much I tell him that it's okay, I'm here for him as much as I am for his sister.

However hard things are for him, he has to be one of the most loyal, loving kids I've ever had the pleasure of knowing. If I'm having one of my bad days, he'll pick up on it almost instantly and surround me with love and hugs, he knows my love language is physical touch, he'll tuck me up in bed and give me one of his cuddly teddy's so that I can nap knowing that he isn't far away.

Because of his neuro-divergence, I've had to learn how to parent him differently. I've taken courses and done groups so that I can better understand his conditions. Learning something different is hard, you have to go against everything that you thought you knew and understood, and flip it. But it's been so worth it. We now live in a house that isn't constantly filled with hostility.

Chapter Thirty-Three

"I think I can. I know I can. I did." — Unknown.

Since Robert and I got together, I have worked really hard on my relationships with my family. It's been hard but I've tried to see situations from their perspective. I'm more than aware I haven't been an easy person to be around.

After I removed myself from the mental health facility, there were some very hard conversations with my parents, they'd been long overdue and desperately needed. It was then, and only then, I realised that most, if not all, of the feelings I'd had leading up to that point had been misplaced.

I think I sulked about it for a year or so, how had I got it so wrong? I'd become entangled in a web of my owns thoughts and feelings and they'd spun me almost out of control.

With Robert by my side, helping me navigate this new normal, I began to see myself how others see me. How my mum and Dad saw me.

Now, at forty-six, I've had the pleasure of many years of love and what can only be described as a fantastic relationship with both of my parents. The love I'd always had, and never seen is in my life in abundance.

Chapter Thirty-Four

"Be your own kind of beautiful." — Unknown.

The whole point of this book, if you've got this far, is to let you know, no matter how hard certain situations may seem, no matter how pointless, you are worth making the choice for. You have something so valuable to offer the world, your family, your friends, that you should always choose to be your best self. It's okay to have bad days, it's okay to feel them, but during those bad days, remember who you are, to yourself and to the people who love you.

One way or another, if you make the choice, like I did, it'll be okay.

Chapter Thirty-Five

Just a little extra.

So the following text, is something my incredible, strong, fourteen-year-old Abie has written. This is from her. It was important to me to add this in here.

I see a good amount of my own story in what my daughter has already been through. She is proving to be resilient and inexplicably strong. She obviously knows I'm writing this, and felt very passionate about adding her part. I hope that you see, like I do, through her words, just how strong she really is.

I'm Abie, I'm 14-years-old. These are just some quick statements about my life and how I've been dealing with some of the things I've gone through.

I love the colour purple because I feel like it's my safe colour. My ultimate favourite music at the moment is Rap, I enjoy listening to Tu Pac, Lil Peep, and Melanie Martinez.

I enjoy binge watching shows like Bob's Burgers and Bones.

My life has been hard, but with help and support, I feel like I'm getting through it.

Wounded.

I've wanted to burn the world, but I mostly wanted to burn them.

I wanted to kill him, instead the rape nearly killed me.

He was like a dog and I got confused, he was cute and kind, but viscous when something didn't go his way.

*A drawing of Beetle
Bug in a grass field.*

Imagine giggling thinking it was a cute game.

If I could throw a tomato at him, it would be the most rotten one.

He was like a fire. I could watch him forever, but I got so close that he burned me.

I was 7 when it first happened and 13 after the last one, I felt like I was failing. It had happened twice, and I couldn't stop it both times, that's hard you know?

It all happened so fast I kept thinking "but did it happen or is my head creating mischief?"

How could I be okay when they stripped my dignity from me?

They were both ignorant, I'm fine, I'm okay but I'm still hurt.

I couldn't have seen what was going to happen, but if I could go back, I would hug little me and say it'll be okay, eventually.

I wanted to sob, but I was so frozen I couldn't remember how.

I can't remember most of my childhood, only the sad memories.

I felt a fire light up inside me, it was so strong it could've burned down a village.

"He wouldn't do that, he's sweet" he literally betrayed my trust with him.

Healing.

Accepting is my best friend, it helped me stop remembering the bad all the time.

I went to war with my head, and I won.

I started to feel better after talking, but it got worse before it got better.

If I needed anything more in my life it would be a Kuchi Kopi and snuggles from my mother.

The more I've healed, the more I realise being a child is the best feeling.

I'm happy, it took a very long time, but I am happy.

I now have the world in my hands, and I'm never letting it go.

Understanding the world was hard, trying to understand why this was all happening to me, did I deserve this? No, I didn't, and neither did anyone else that's reading this. You are strong and you are going to get through it, but it takes hard work and faith in yourself.

It was my choice to go to his house and trust him, but it was his choice to do what he did, that doesn't mean it was my fault.

I've accepted that I didn't and don't have the control over the choice he made, could it have been better? Yes, but it wasn't so here I am, living my best life.

If I could be anyone, I'd be my mother, she's strong, kind, and beautiful, but most importantly she's showed me accepting isn't as hard as I was making it out to be, I was scared, but she held me through the tough times and she is the woman I aspire to be when I grow up.

Forgiving was the hardest part, I could forgive the little boy, but not him.

I felt like I was dying on the inside, but really it was the start of the best bit of my life.

I was a clam hidden in the deep waters, my beautiful pearl on the inside when it was really my heart blossoming waiting for the right person to come along and treasure me.

Never believe that you are at fault because of what happened to you because you aren't, you are awesome.

Believe in yourself, think about the future.

You thought you were a boring moth, but in reality, you are a beautiful butterfly who couldn't see their wings.

Don't be the fire, be the water that helps it calm down.

The masking was and is easy, but healing made me not want to do it anymore.

You might wonder who the purple and green bug looking thing is, that's Beetle Bug! They are my trauma superhero, they save me from my trauma so I can't think about it happening. Beetle Bug is my story's saviour, and everyone needs one of those. I'm currently working on a comic book for them and Beetle Bug's superhero friends!

CHAPTER THIRTY-SIX

Acknowledgements

Thank you doesn't seem to quite cover what I want to say. But I'll give it a go anyway.

Mum and Dad, I know I haven't been an easy person to live with while I was growing up. So, I'm sorry for everything that I put you through. Dad got it right, I learned how to join the human race somewhere around twenty-seven. Thank you for loving me anyway and staying right by my side. I love you.

Robert, you're my rock. My husband, soulmate, and best friend. I couldn't have got nearly as far in life if it hadn't been for you. I love you with everything I am, and I can't wait for this next adventure that we're doing together. You keep me grounded, Rabbit and I am so thankful for you while you've encouraged me to be on this journey. I haven't been an easy person at the best of times to be around. So thank you.

ACWM and ARM, God gave me the best present when he gave you to me. I know life hasn't been easy for either of you, but when I tell you that I couldn't be any prouder of you, I mean it. You are both what gets me up in the morning, and what I think about when I go to sleep. I love you, my babies.

Jeanne, I love you. I am so grateful for your friendship. You've talked me off several ledges and made me see sense when I couldn't find it. I'm so grateful for you. Thank you.

Andi, you're a fucking rockstar. I'm so glad that it was you behind me in that line for Portland. You are a forever type of friend and I adore you.

Perry, without the things that you are doing and accomplishing, this book would never have made the light of day. You gave me the final push I needed. Thank you doesn't come close, but it will have to do. Who knew I'd be able to say that I've had lunch with a famous actor.

Bonnie, Jacqui, Aly, Rose, Glenn, Scott, Debbra, Dianelba and every other person in our group, thank you all for supporting me and my no bullshit ways and for loving me just the way I am. You are all incredible and I love you all.